Becoming God's Beloved
in the Company of Friends

Becoming God's Beloved
in the Company of Friends

—————— *A Spirituality of the Fourth Gospel* ——————

Mary Margaret Pazdan, OP

CASCADE *Books* · Eugene, Oregon

BECOMING GOD'S BELOVED
IN THE COMPANY OF FRIENDS
A Spirituality of the Fourth Gospel

Cascade Books
A Division of Wipf and Stock Publishers
199 W. 8th Ave., Suite 3
Eugene, OR 97401

ISBN 13: 978-1-55635-462-5

Cataloging-in-Publication data:

Pazdan, Mary Margaret.
Becoming God's beloved in the company of friends : a spirituality of the fourth gospel / by Mary Margaret Pazdan, OP.

viii + 126p. ; 20 cm.

ISBN 13: 978-1-55635-462-5

1. Bible. N.T. John—Criticism, interpretation, etc. 2. Bible. N.T. John—Theology. 3. Spirituality—Biblical teaching. I. Title.

BS2615.2 P38 2007

Manufactured in the U.S.A.

In loving memory of my parents,
Eugenia and Edward Pazdan,
God's beloved in the company of friends

Contents

List of Charts

Introduction

The Gospel of John and I have been companions since I received a gift for Christmas in 1961 when I was a novice at the Sinsinawa Dominican Motherhouse in Wisconsin. It was Raymond E. Brown's first commentary on the Gospel. During these last four decades I have discovered that the Fourth Gospel is a mysterious book that believers have been encountering in prayer, study, and preaching for two millennia with no sign of flagging interest. A second-century Gnostic, Heracleon, was the first person to write a commentary about the Gospel in the second century.[1] Throughout orthodox Christian history, too, theologians and preachers (for example, Augustine, Thomas Aquinas, Catherine of Siena), as well as contemporary biblical scholars, have found in the Gospel an invitation to the spiritual life that is mysterious, challenging, and transforming.

A Mysterious Gospel

Why is the Fourth Gospel mysterious? Jesus does not speak like the "Jesus" of Matthew, Mark, or Luke. He always takes the initiative and asks many questions, from his first words to the disciples of John the Baptist (1:38) to his last questions

1. Pagels, *The Johannine Gospel in Gnostic Exegesis.*

after the resurrection to Mary Magdalene (20:13), Thomas
(20:29), the disciples (21:5), and Peter (21:15–17, 22). The
characters, however, are not sure how to answer. Ordinarily,
they respond quickly but with little insight. Jesus, however,
asks a question because he wants to begin a relationship if
an individual is willing to believe in him. The Book of Signs
(John 1–12) is a drama of how Jesus invites different characters to believe in him, to make a decision, to take a risk,
because of what he says or does.

Jesus not only asks many questions, but he also encourages a dialogue so that an individual's customary ways of
speaking and acting as a Jew or Gentile can be turned upside
down. Remember, for example, Nicodemus who comes to
him at night (3:1–21) and the woman of Samaria who encounters him in the blistering sunlight (4:4–26).

Nonetheless, the power of a dialogue with Jesus does not
happen for an individual alone. Rather, the encounter impels
an individual to share the experience. Witnessing the Jesus experience to another is a risk. It is taking a chance of touching
the soul of another and asking for acceptance or rejection on
the word of another. In the Fourth Gospel, it is the beginning
of being a disciple in the company of others.

Sometimes Jesus' dialogue with an individual or group
becomes a monologue. When Jesus feeds the five thousand on
the hillside and walks on the water (6:1–21), he startles a large
crowd and the disciples with his teaching (6:22–58). Think
about the paralytic at the pool in Bethsaida (5:1–47) or the
raising of Lazarus (11:1–44). In the Book of Glory (chapters
13–20), Jesus begins a conversation that quickly turns into

an extended monologue with only a few questions from the disciples (13:1—17:26).

Again, the Johannine Jesus is mysterious because he acts differently than does the Synoptic Jesus. Jesus performs seven signs (*sēmeia*) with teaching so that persons may glimpse his identity. A comparison of the Synoptic Gospels' twenty-seven miracles to the signs of the Fourth Gospel indicates several narratives with parallels, i.e., paralytics, blind persons, and the centurion's son (servant). However, only one story, the feeding on the hillside, relates theologically to the synoptic accounts of the Last Supper and the Bread of Life discourse. Jesus also spends more time and energy during his ministry in Judea, especially Jerusalem, unlike the Synoptic Jesus who visits Jerusalem only one time.

A Challenging Gospel

The distinctive portrait of Jesus, especially his manner of speaking and acting, challenges believers today. Sometimes, when we study and pray about a *pericope*, i.e., a short selection of the Gospel like a lectionary text, we are not sure what is happening. The first challenge to the reader is that Jesus speaks and acts like a first-century Jew whose culture embodies particular values of honor (purity) and shame (pollution or sin). What is at stake for Jesus is the honor of his household. Jesus speaks as the Beloved Son of the Father by declaring what he has heard from the Father (8:38). In his dialogue with various characters, especially the Pharisees, Jesus listens, challenges, and replies. While Jesus' language may appear harsh and condemnatory, unless he acts with integrity in these private and public situations, his Father will be shamed. The challenge-riposte custom is the principal venue for honor and shame in Mediterranean culture.

How did people of the Mediterranean attribute honor and shame to one another? If an individual was not a complete, physical being, he and his whole household were sinners. Each person in the Mediterranean world consisted of three personality zones. The first zone was eyes-heart to indicate what a person thinks. Reflect on the story of the man born blind in chapter 9. Recall the conversations with the Pharisees, the parents, Jesus. The second zone was the ears-mouth for communication. The third zone was the hands-feet for purposeful action. Think of the official's son who was at the point of death (4:46–54): his condition meant no personality zone could be operative.

During Jesus' time, people believed that God could restore people to wholeness since God's power was stronger than the demonic power of illness and disease. In the Gospel, Jesus, as God's beloved son, functions as the intermediary or broker for the people to break the power of evil. God, whom Jesus addresses as Father, is the benefactor or patron of whatever promotes life in everything Jesus says and does.

A second challenge of the Gospel is how to respond to the claims of anti-Jewish bias. In Christian tradition, *hoi Ioudaioi* is translated as "the Jews." Many believers argue that *hoi Ioudaioi* is used derogatively and promotes anti-Semitic attitudes in the church. Others find that the Johannine Passion Narrative is difficult to proclaim in Christian churches on Good Friday. Today, linguistic, cultural and theological studies offer us additional perspectives.[2]

---

2. For comprehensive and current perspectives, see Bieringer et al.,

Recently, Fred Danker, a distinguished Greek and New Testament scholar, pointed out that *hoi Ioudaioi* identifies "the Judeans," a group who lived in southern Israel. It is inappropriate to translate the term in order to project religious identity instead of a geographical designation.[3] Similarly, cultural anthropologists point out that it is incongruous to project contemporary meanings of "Jew" or "Jewishness" to the period when the Gospel was written.[4]

Some point to the Johannine community as the source of the bias. Their situation, however, is complex. As a small sect of Jewish believers in Jesus, they developed a language system and a method of arguing that may sound offensive and harsh to contemporary ears. After the collapse of the Temple in 70 CE, the community was struggling for identity vis-à-vis the authoritative Pharisees and their groups whose followers were codifying laws about what constitutes faithful Jewish living before God.

The polemical language, especially of chapters 5, 7, and 8, is a cultural expression about how the Johannine community is claiming its identity as a small minority who challenges first-century Judaism. Their integrity includes claiming their identity as Jews who earnestly desire dialogue with the Pharisees about Jesus. Unfortunately, these chapters have often been interpreted theologically with no consideration of the language system of the first-century Mediterranean world.

---

editors, *Anti-Judaism and the Fourth Gospel.*

3. Danker in an online interview about his seven-year editing of the standard lexicon, Bauer, et al., *A Greek-English Lexicon of the New Testament,* June 14, 2001.

4. Malina and Rohrbaugh, *Social-Science Commentary on the Gospel of John,* 44–46.

In addition, it is difficult to separate out what group of Pharisees Jesus is addressing in the Gospel. Sometimes the scene reflects the Jesus of Judea. At other times, it describes the Johannine community's experience of Jesus and their situation of post-Temple dialogue. The sharp retorts that Jesus offers to the Pharisees' questions are a matter of honor. The language of the Gospel indicates a small Israelite community living outside of greater Palestine, probably in Ephesus, that resists the values of the dominant society, i.e., "the world," "the Judeans."[5]

The dualistic language of the Gospel is also problematic in understanding *hoi Ioudaioi*. The language reflects the either-or cultural code of honor and shame. It also hints at a type of early Gnostic thought, whereby the heavenly and spiritual are more valuable than the earthly and physical. The dualistic language hinges on the question of how persons relate to Jesus. To believe in Jesus is to be in the light; conversely, to not believe is to be in darkness. Believing is the basic commitment toward becoming a member of the household of God, a beloved daughter or son.

While many Judeans did not believe in Jesus (12:36–43), some did believe (8:31; 12:42). Symbolically, *hoi Ioudaioi*, especially the Pharisees, represent all who live in darkness, the nonbelievers. It is important, however, to see that there is freedom of choice to believe, not to believe, or to change one's decision about believing in Jesus (cf. 3:17–21). The Gospel does not condemn ethnic and religious Jews as incapable of

5. See the description of anti-society and anti-language features of the Johannine community in Malina and Rohrbaugh, *John*, 4–10.

salvation. Rather, it does claim the centrality of believing in Jesus.

A third challenge is the "Father-Son" and "Son of Man" language in the Fourth Gospel. These designations can appear painful and exclusive and are difficult to negotiate in teaching, preaching, liturgy, and prayer. Acknowledging the metaphorical nature of theological language as well as the implications of the Father-Son paradigm does not always alleviate the questions for believers. Communal study, formation, and appropriation are necessary to respond pastorally in any area that affects the vitality of church life.

A fourth challenge that we inherit is a lurking shadow when we consider spirituality today. We encounter the major stories in the Gospel as meetings of individuals with Jesus. They appear unrelated to vital justice issues. The Gospel includes no mention of the beatitudes that Matthew and Luke articulate. We do not find narratives of rich and poor persons that Luke–Acts describes so eloquently. The memory of the Markan Jesus who moves quickly and decisively in his relationships with crowds who expect the end of the world is missing. The Johannine Jesus speaks and acts from a contemplative way of being that is difficult for us activists. Nevertheless, encounter with this mysterious and challenging Jesus can move us to be transformed for service in the church if we are open to change.

A Transforming Gospel

Prayer and study in dialogue with the Fourth Gospel and others can be an experience of ongoing transformation for believers today. These vital activities are the basis for becoming

God's beloved in the company of friends. I combine "becoming God's beloved" with "in the company of friends" because of several theological dynamics. First, according to Henri J. M. Nouwen, "We are the Beloved. . . . That's the truth of our lives."[6] Our spiritual journey is to claim our identity, i.e., "the origin and the fulfillment of the life of the Spirit."[7]

Second, in the Fourth Gospel, Jesus is the Father's Beloved in a mutual life of knowing, loving, and abiding. The call to be a disciple is the call to claim personal identity as beloved in a distinctive life-long path. Believing in Jesus initiates an individual into the shared life of Jesus and the Father. The Spirit, the gift of Jesus and the Father, enables a disciple to be witness, to be a presence of the beloved for others (20:19–24). The mysterious appearances of the Beloved Disciple can be interpreted as another model of witness and presence (13:23–25; 19:25–27; 21:20–25).

Third, "in the company of friends" describes the modality of living as beloved, as disciples. Being God's beloved necessitates relationship. A community of believers is fundamental to developing this identity. In a recent monograph, Sharon H. Ringe traces the development of classical themes of "wisdom" and "friendship" to their climax in the relationships of Jesus and the disciples of the Fourth Gospel. In particular, we see how "friends" is the context and depth of Jesus' radical command to the disciples:

> This is my commandment, that you love one another as I have loved you. No one has greater love than this, to lay down one's life for one's friends. You are my friends if you do what I command you.

6. Nouwen, *Life of the Beloved,* 30.
7. Ibid., 37.

> I do not call you servants any longer, because the
> servant does not know what the master is doing;
> but I have called you friends, because I have made
> known to you everything that I have heard from my
> Father. (15:12–15, NRSV)

In fact, this passage functions "as a lens through which to
view the theme in the Fourth Gospel as a whole."[8] The company of friends, however, is not self-absorbed and exclusive.
It is a distinctive way of life "to bear fruit, fruit that will last"
(15:16b).

Outline of the Book

This book is not a traditional, spiritual commentary on the
Gospel of John. It does not offer a line-by-line interpretation
of the text. Rather, it describes the process of how one becomes
a disciple of Jesus, God's beloved. Chapter 1 considers believing in Jesus as the initial commitment in becoming a disciple.
Chapter 2 describes the mutual life of Jesus and the Father
as knowing, loving, and abiding in one another. Chapter 3
develops how the beloved experience mutual knowing, loving, and abiding in the household of God. Chapters 4 and 5
present activities of God's beloved in the household of God,
namely, hearing and keeping Jesus' word as well as seeking
and finding him.

Each chapter focuses on a few stories and a few teachings
to illustrate a particular characteristic of becoming a disciple.
Other narratives and instructions are noted in less detail to develop a theme, e.g., believing in Jesus. This approach enables
readers to become familiar with how the Gospel is written

8. Ringe, *Wisdom's Friends*, 65.

in a spiral whereby particular theological themes are repeated several times in different sections of the Gospel.

Structure of the Chapters

Each chapter has three parts that serve as a bridge across time from first-century- to twenty-first-century disciples. Becoming God's beloved is integrally connected with becoming disciples of Jesus. First, *Reflection Questions* engage readers with personal experience of the dynamic of discipleship. The questions enable us to take an inventory of memories that continue to form us in our spiritual journey. It is in the First Naiveté where each of us connects mind and heart with personal experience for reading a text. Naiveté does not mean a lack of sophistication or unfamiliarity. Rather, we approach a familiar text with curiosity to read and hear something new, like a child or an individual who is familiar with certain stories but wants to hear them again.

Next, readers are asked to pursue *Critical Inquiry of Christian Tradition* for interpretation of a text. This process includes dialogue with two groups of scholars. First, we engage biblical theologians from the early and medieval church, especially Thomas Aquinas. His *Catena Aurea* is a running commentary on all four Gospels, culled from the Fathers of the Church. His *Commentary on the Gospel of John* is another source. I also quote some writings of Catherine of Siena who loved the mystical images and metaphors of the Gospel of John. The retrieval of this heritage enables us to understand how vital biblical revelation was to early theologians who exerted no small effort in preaching and lecturing on the Gospel of John. Their understanding of the literal meaning of a text as well as spiritual insights for life in the church (for example, Christology and Sacramental life) offer new insights and remarkable nuances for the Gospel.

We also will bring contemporary scholars into conversation, in order to offer readers deep and broad horizons for reflection. These interpreters will represent the wide horizons of interpretation that are emerging as the hegemony of the historical-critical method gives way to the acceptance of liberationist criticism today.[9] Reading from diverse theological authors may refresh and broaden readers' intuition and experience.

In reading from a variety of interpreters, the reader will experience distanciation. This is the experience of finding oneself in a situation where familiarity with the text is expanded by the new insights of the interpreters or where personal understanding does not find a home with other interpretations. Distanciation breaks open a reader's familiarity with a text by confronting the reader with a surplus of meaning that challenges personal understanding. Sometimes, it is as though one is reading the text again for the first time.

Finally, there is the challenge of *Appropriation*. How does being attentive to the personal inventory (*First Naiveté*) and *Critical Inquiry* of Christian Tradition call us to be challenged, and changed, by a particular experience of becoming God's beloved? How are we to be given the insight to

9. The Pontifical Biblical Commission issued a document, "The Interpretation of the Bible in the Church," to Pope John Paul II on April 23, 1993; it was published in *Origins*. The document considers methods, hermeneutical questions, characteristics of Catholic interpretation, and how the Bible is interpreted in the life of the church. It parallels other contributions in the academy. For the document and bibliography, see Béchard, ed. and trans., *The Scripture Documents*, 244–73.

proclaim the Jesus story with new understanding? This is the Second Naiveté, in which our encounter with the text calls for the courage to internalize new insights and to be willing to witness them for others. Witness or testimony is essential in living a Christian life.

Please read through the entire Gospel before beginning the chapters of the book. It helps to re-familiarize oneself again with the Gospel in its entirety rather than to be content with snippets or favorite passages or lectionary pericopes. By using the energies of mind and heart in prayerful reading, we allow familiar stories to challenge us and we open ourselves to transformation.

Readers will discover that the heart of the process is dialogue with oneself and others to deepen and expand the authenticity of the spiritual journey. If the chapters can be used in small groups, the dialogue can move in surprising and strengthening directions. The Spirit enables the entire process as she equips readers with individual and various gifts for personal transformation (1 Cor 12:4–7).

Feast of St. Catherine of Siena
April 29, 2007

---—— I ——---

Believing in Jesus

The First Commitment toward Becoming God's Beloved

Believing in anyone takes a soupcon of trust, courage, and chutzpah. Sometimes it is the mere presence of a person and what that person says or does that inspires us to desire a relationship. We feel an intuition, a simpatico, or a click that urges us to speak or stretch out a hand to another. At other times, we hear about a person and we are curious. We are not content either to second-guess for ourselves or to trust the word of someone else. We need to experience the person who is being spoken about for ourselves before we even imagine a relationship.

Believing in another person also entails the risk of discovering ourselves in a new way. We learn who we are with our gifts and limitations through the trust we have in another to identify us. Being open and being vulnerable are implicit when we begin to believe in another and hope for a genuine relationship. Especially as adults, it can be intimidating to simply hold out our perceptions of self to another for acceptance or rejection.

Reflection Questions: First Naiveté

1. What is your earliest experience of another person? Recall the event by engaging your senses to re-imagine it as an adult. Write down several phrases that express how your body, mind, and spirit felt. Draw a picture to capture the experience. You may be able to tell the story to another person if you are studying the Gospel of John together.

2. What is your most recent experience of another person? Review the event by referring to question 1. Compare and contrast the experiences to discover if there are any similarities.

3. What is your earliest experience of God? Follow the suggestions of question 1.

4. What is your most recent experience of God? Follow question 1.

5. Reflect upon the Gospel of John. Can you name any characters who believe in Jesus? Why? How do you know? Are they loyal and faithful to Jesus?

6. Now read John 1:1–18, the Prologue. Is there any word, phrase, or image that is similar to your responses for questions 1–5? If so, write them down.

7. Finally, review questions 1–6. Read John 1:19–51. What happens?

Critical Inquiry of Christian Tradition
Prologue (1:1–18)

"In the beginning" before we can imagine time, there are the Word and God (John 1:1). Who knows how God calibrates time? For example, Jeremiah hears God speaking: "Before I formed you in the womb, I knew you, and before you were born I consecrated you; I appointed you a prophet to the nations" (Jer 1:4). What is "before" for us? In contrast, when we read our first book of sacred history, Genesis, we can trace the cosmic beginning of God's initiative when the earth was dark with no shape (Gen 1:1). The Genesis creation accounts describe the shaping of the cosmos and human beings (Gen 1:1–31; 2:1–25).

In the Prologue of John (vv. 1–18), however, we ponder another insight about time and creation. This extraordinary hymn offers us a glimpse about God's time and providence. In God's time, "in the beginning," there are God and the Word (vv. 1–2). Both create all life as light for all people that no darkness can overwhelm (vv. 3–5). The Word is Light to which John bears witness (vv. 6–8). The Word became flesh, and his presence is like the *Shekinah*, the glory of God that the Hebrews experienced in the wilderness (v. 14). It is the Word as God's Beloved Son who dwells among the people offering them life and light. God and the Word made flesh dwell with one another. The Beloved Son lives at the heart of the Father (v. 18).

How did the Johannine community create the hymn to the Word? What heritage did members draw upon from their memories and imaginations? They reflected upon a mysterious figure named Wisdom: *Ḥokmah* (Hebrew) or *Sophia* (Greek).

In particular, they pondered particular qualities of Wisdom that enable her to be in relationship with the cosmos, human beings, and God.

First, Wisdom is an abiding presence that hearts and minds and souls long for throughout life (Prov 3:13–15). She is more valuable than all human efforts, achievements, and dreams; yet the Lady is elusive like quicksilver (cf. Prov 2:4). She is not to be possessed through expending and expanding energies searching for her. Why? Sophia always takes the initiative. She whispers in attentive ears, "Seek me. Come to me."

Second, Wisdom is pure gift. Her presence and absence are easy to experience but difficult to accept. Wisdom is not like a reliable income to draw upon in critical moments. Wisdom is not accessible through solitary pleas; Wisdom comes in God's time.

Third, Wisdom is never found in isolation. Wisdom breathes, speaks, walks, and moves only in relationships. Her traces appear in relationships with God, among families, friends, and neighbors, in spider webs, starry skies and ocean foam. Wisdom is revealed wherever and whenever relationships speak and witness to the possibilities and limitations of human lives. Wisdom, like God, calls every person to life (Prov 1:23, 25, 30; 8:6–9, 15, 35). Since Wisdom was present at creation (Prov 8:22–31), she proclaims to all, "whoever finds me finds life and obtains favor from the Lord" (Prov 8:35).

Fourth, Wisdom nourishes life. She invites all into her house of seven pillars: "Come, eat of my bread and drink of the wine I have mixed. Lay aside immaturity and live, and walk in the way of insight" (Prov 9:5–6). Wisdom's bounty is available, "Come to me, you who desire me, and eat your fill of my fruits" (Sir 24:19).

Fifth, Wisdom renews and transforms creation because of her extraordinary relationship with God. "While remaining in herself, she renews all things; in every generation she passes into holy souls and makes them friends of God, and prophets; for God loves nothing so much as the person who lives with wisdom" (Wis 7:27–28).

In the Prologue, we discover the culmination of the Wisdom tradition, "The Word became flesh and dwelled among us, and we have seen his glory, the glory as of a father's only Son, full of grace and truth" (v. 14). Jesus was the Wisdom of God for the Johannine community and believers.

Narrative Scenes (1:19–51)

Now we turn to the prose section of chapter 1. Here we find persons interacting with others and Jesus. See chart 1.1 **Prologue (1:1–18) and Narrative Scenes (1:19–51)** on the next page. Notice that John 1:19–51 is a series of seven narrative scenes. When we read through the *settings,* do they fill in adequate details of place and time? The common setting is Galilee in northern Israel. Exact time is not important since Mediterranean people lived in the present moment. The narrator only mentions "the next day" (vv. 29, 35, 43) and "four o'clock in the afternoon" (v. 39).

What about the list of *characters*? Some remain for a few scenes while others disappear, like the priests and Pharisees. *Named* characters are often more important in a scene than *unnamed* persons, groups, or crowds. A community remem-

CHART 1.1

Prologue: (1:1-18)

POETRY AND PROSE (vv. 6-8, 15)

Narrative Scenes (1:19-51)

Scene One. 1:19-28.	Scene Two. 1:29-34.	Scene Three. 1:35-39.
SETTING "Bethany across the Jordan where John was preaching" (v. 28)	*SETTING* "The next day" (v. 29)	*SETTING* "The next day" (v. 35) "four o'clock in the afternoon" (v. 39)
CHARACTERS "John . . . Jews . . . priests . . . Levites" (v. 19) "Pharisees" (v. 24)	*CHARACTERS* "Jesus" (v. 29) "he . . . John " (vv. 29, 32) John as "I" (vv. 31, 32, 33, 34)	*CHARACTERS* "John" "two of his disciples" (v. 35) "Jesus" (v. 36).
CONFLICTS Who is John? By whose authority does he baptize?	*CONFLICTS* Hearers and readers may question John's authority and he testified about Jesus' identity.	*CONFLICTS* Will disciples trust John's witness? Will they follow someone greater than he? (v. 15). Will they respond to his challenges? (vv. 38–39).
DENOUEMENT *John* speaks the truth about his identity (v. 23; cf. 1:6-8). He describes one whom they do not **know** (vv. 26–27; cf. 1:15). His testimony is reliable.	*DENOUEMENT* ". . . *the one who sent me to baptize with water*: He on whom you see the Spirit descend and **remain** is *the one who baptizes with the Holy Spirit*" (v. 33). *John*: "I myself have seen and have testified that this is the **Son of God**" (v. 34).	*DENOUEMENT* John loses two disciples. Basic human questions: "**What are you looking for?** . . . **Where are you staying?**" (v. 38). The *disciples* respond to *Jesus'* invitation: "**Come and see** . . . They **remained** with him" (v. 39).

Note: This chart is a visual tool for understanding the drama of the seven narrative scenes in chapter 1. The italicized words signify narrative components of the scene and the characters. The bold words indicate theological terms that are important throughout the Gospel.

(Continuation of Narrative Scenes)

Scene 4. 1:40–42.	Scene 5. 1:43–44.	Scene 6. 1:45–46	Scene 7. 1:47–51.
SETTING "Four o'clock in the afternoon" (v. 39)	**SETTING** "Galilee"(v. 43)	**SETTING** "Nazareth" (vv. 45-46)	**SETTING** Same
CHARACTERS "Andrew, Simon Peter's brother" (v. 40), **natural kinship,** "Simon" (vv. 41, 42), "Simon, son of John … Cephas (which is translated Peter)" (v. 42), "Jesus" (v. 42)	**CHARACTERS** "Jesus … Philip" (v. 43)	**CHARACTERS** Philip …Nathanael (vv. 44-45) Bethsaida is the **social identity** of Simon Peter, Andrew and Philip (v. 44).	**CHARACTERS** "Jesus … Nathanael (v. 47)
CONFLICTS What is the relationship between the brothers? Will Simon **believe** Andrew's witness: "We have **found** the **Messiah**" (v. 41; cf. v. 38)? Will Simon accept a new name from a stranger? (v. 42)	**CONFLICTS** Why does Jesus find Philip (v.43)? What does Philip **know** about Jesus' identity and authority? Will Philip follow? (v. 44)	**CONFLICTS** Why does Philip **find** Nathanael? What does Philip **know** about him? Where does his authority to testify about Jesus originate? "We have **found** him about **whom Moses in the law and also the prophets wrote …"** (v. 45). Will Nathanael accept "Jesus, son of Joseph from Nazareth"? (v. 45).	**CONFLICTS** Why does Nathanael **come** to Jesus? How does Jesus **know** him? What does Nathanael **know** about him? Where does his authority to testify to Jesus about his identity originate: "**Rabbi,** you are the **Son of God** You are the **king of Israel!**" (v. 49)? What does Jesus mean about seeing greater things if Nathanael **believes?** (v. 50)
DENOUEMENT Andrew speaks and appears first in the narrative. His experience of Jesus gives him insight into his identity that he witnesses to his brother. *He brings Simon to share his experience.*	**DENOUEMENT** Unresolved conflicts in the scene.	**DENOUEMENT** Philip counters his skepticism: **"Come and see"** (v. 46).	**DENOUEMENT** Jesus **knows** Nathanael is a genuine Israelite with no guile (v. 47). His knowledge comes from seeing him under a fig tree before Philip called him (v. 48).

bered persons and handed down their significance through story.

A strict gender-based division of work existed in the Mediterranean world. Notice that the characters have male names. Maintaining *honor* is the responsibility of the head of the household, a male, who enters the public arena to guard and maintain it through dialogue with other males. *Shame* is positive, virtuous living, i.e., the integrity of household, for which females are responsible. Women nurture values among the members of the household in domestic situations.

Let us consider the *conflicts* section. The essential conflict in each scene is: Whose authority counts? Why should another's testimony be trusted? As conscientious readers, we are in the same situation as the characters. Whose authority do we trust to hand down and interpret the Jesus story? I highlight the verbs in bold print. They are significant words that have many levels of meaning. Important characters are italicized.

The fourth section in each scene is labeled *Denouement*, i.e., the ending or resolution of conflicts. However, the characters do not always resolve conflicts by the end of the scene, e.g., 1:43–44. Sometimes, characters disappear and we do not know what happens to the conflict, e.g., 3:11–21.

How does the narrative structure of each scene disclose theological insights? Whose authority counts was an important question to maintain the honor of one's household in the first-century Mediterranean world. Each day the head of the household went out to meet another male. The partners addressed one another with sharply focused questions and responses to discover the answer about authority.

SCENE ONE (vv. 19–28)

The Pharisees send priests and Levites to John because they are curious about his authority to baptize (v. 19). They may have heard through the active gossip network, the traditional way news traveled from village to village, that some people thought he might be the Messiah, Elijah, or the prophet of the end time. John speaks his own truth, but they want more. In verse 22, we see that they are envoys (brokers) for the Pharisees, the adjudicators of purity laws. John ascribes his authority to baptize "to one whom they do not know" (v. 26). There is no response to his reliable witness. We can only imagine what the Pharisees thought about the information.

SCENE TWO (vv. 29–34)

In contrast to the first scene, this scene describes John's experience of seeing Jesus. John functions as a prophet for the crowd. He names Jesus as "the Lamb of God who takes away the sin of the world" (v. 29) so that he may be revealed to Israel (v. 31). There is no longer any need for repeated water rituals of public cleansing for sin. John's vision authenticates his words: "I saw the Spirit descending from heaven like a dove, and it remained on him" (v. 32). Jesus baptizes with the Holy Spirit (v. 33). John's final witness in the Gospel echoes the Prologue: "Jesus is the Son of God" (v. 34, cf. v. 18). Who gave John authority to name Jesus? How do listeners respond? Readers wait expectantly for Jesus' and the crowd's response. Neither replies. Perhaps some of his disciples listen to his witness (v. 35) that he repeats the next day in scene 3 (vv. 35–36).

SCENE THREE (vv. 35–39)

Whatever the power and content of his witness may be, we know that John loses two disciples to Jesus (v. 37). Is he shamed? His only role is to witness to the light (vv. 7–8). Nonetheless, there is probably rivalry between the followers of John and Jesus (see 4:1).

When Jesus looks around, he invites two unnamed persons to a challenge. His question is the basic one of the spiritual life, "What are you looking for?" or as some Greek manuscripts suggest, "Whom are you looking for?" Instead, they ask him a question, "Where are you staying?" (v. 38). Jesus invites them, "Come and see." They follow, see, and stay with him (v. 39). It is an example of Johannine irony or misunderstanding. Readers know that "staying" or "abiding" suggest a mysterious relationship.

SCENE FOUR (vv. 40–42)

What do the two former disciples of John experience of Jesus? How do they experience him? The narrator does not offer us biographical details. Rather, Andrew rushes out to invite his brother to share the experience of knowing Jesus as Messiah, not simply as another Rabbi (vv. 40–41, cf. v. 38). When he is hesitant, Andrew brings Simon to Jesus. In the Synoptic Gospels, Andrew does not function as a special character. He is a shadow to Peter whose single appearance in the Gospels is one of two brothers whom Jesus calls first (Matthew 4:18–22; Mark 1:16–20).

What about Simon? Unlike the loquacious character that we encounter later, here he is silent. His new name, "Cephas," identifies him as a member of a new family. In the Mediterranean world, persons do not have individual identity. Rather, they function in relationship to others, i.e., dyadic personality. Fictive kinship offers individuals new dyadic relationships to others who freely associate with one another. They form a new household (cf. Matthew 12:46–50; Mark 3:31–35; Luke 8:19–21). Cephas has fictive kinship with Jesus, his brother Andrew, and all who are called to be disciples.

Scene Five (vv. 43–44)

Something new happens here. Jesus takes the initiative to set out for Galilee, *find* Philip and call him to belong to the new fictive kin group. Philip does not reply. However, he responds like Andrew by going out to find Nathanael. In this short scene, we also learn that three members of the new household, i.e., Andrew, Cephas, and Philip are from Bethsaida in Galilee (v. 44).

Geographical location is another social identity label. For Torah-observant Jews, one's geographical location is closely associated with purity (holiness) or pollution (sin). The region of Samaria is forbidden as a residence because of centuries of religious conflict over the Temple and Law. Galilee is better than Samaria, but its distance from the Temple in Jerusalem renders Galileans suspect. Their attitudes toward intermarriage, distrust of Jerusalem officials, and the temple tax violate many purity laws. The best place to live is Judea, especially Jerusalem near the Temple, the center of holiness.

Holiness is a basic value for the Jewish people. They devote attention, devotion, and effort to preserve God's holiness with complex religious laws about the Temple, the dwelling of God. Correspondingly, they are also concerned about their holiness. Extensive laws reflect what constitutes human holiness as well as what violates holiness and boundaries.

The geographical markers in chapter 1 are holiness boundaries. While the first four scenes occur in Judea, the persons who are called to be disciples are from Galilee.

SCENE SIX (VV. 45–46)

Witnessing from one's experience sometimes meets resistance. Philip's enthusiastic witness to Nathanael about Jesus is hampered by his geographical reference: "Jesus the Son of Joseph from Nazareth." Although Philip proclaims him as the fulfillment of the Law and Prophets, Nathanael only hears "Nazareth" (in Galilee). In a typical challenge-riposte style, Nathanael replies, "Can anything good come out of Nazareth?" Philip echoes Jesus' invitation to Andrew and the other disciple, "Come and see" (1:39).

SCENE SEVEN (VV. 47–51)

The narrator does not even give Nathanael time to make a decision. Suddenly, Jesus is coming toward him. He praises him as an Israelite "in whom there is no deceit" (v. 47). How does Jesus know Nathanael? The enigmatic response, "I saw you sitting under a fig tree" (v. 50), is another example of drawing upon the Hebrew Scriptures. A fig tree is often a symbol of peace and being at home (1 Kings 4:25; Isaiah 36:16; cf. Matthew 21:18–19; Mark 11:12–14). Micah and Zechariah proclaim God's future as a time when families will sit down under their own vines and fig trees (Micah 4:4; Zechariah 3:10). In this context, Jesus knows of Nathanael's household but he will show him another home, a fictive kinship.

Jesus' "knowing" and "seeing" Nathanael are challenges to his believing in him.

Nathanael assumes the challenge and witnesses to Jesus' divine origin, "Son of God," and his mission, "King of Israel" (v. 48). While "Son of God" is repeated throughout the Gospel as a positive identification of Jesus, the recognition of "King of Israel" is disputed between Pilate and the Judeans (19:3–21).

Jesus has the final word in the scene. He promises Nathanael that he will experience greater things than their present conversation. "You will see heaven opened and the angels of God ascending and descending upon the Son of Man" (v. 51). When we look at the names that others give Jesus throughout the seven scenes, we may be puzzled by Jesus' preference for his self-identity as "Son of Man." The metaphor that frames his identity presents a new insight. The incarnate Word is the one whose being is the divine presence as well as the access to God.

Other Catalysts for Believing in Jesus

The primary question for individuals and crowds who encounter Jesus is: Do you believe (*pisteueis*)? The question is developed in many ways. The narrative scenes of chapter 1 indicate that a person's witness is what draws another to believe in Jesus initially. The second step is a personal experience of Jesus that more than confirms the witness. There are other catalysts for believing in Jesus in the Book of Signs, too, namely, the signs (*sēmeia*), other witnesses, and human freedom. The literary device of *foil characters* plays an important role for readers. Each relationship that an individual or group seeks with Jesus also has an opposite possibility. The narrator uses the same verb and a negative modifier for the foil character who neither believes in Jesus (3:18) nor comes to him (3:20). A *foil character* refuses to accept the *sēmeia* and other witnesses and thereby exercises personal freedom to not believe in Jesus.

Who are the foil characters in the Fourth Gospel? Those who do not believe in Jesus live among the same individuals and groups who believe in Jesus, i.e., Jesus' contemporaries and those living after the resurrection. The use of the indefinite subject, "one," as well as the symbolic nature of certain characters that appear in the Gospel, namely, Jesus' brothers, the Judeans, and the world identify them for readers.

THE SĒMEIA NARRATIVES

There are seven *sēmeia* narratives in the Book of Signs: changing water into wine (2:1–11), healing of the royal official's son (4:46–54), healing of the paralytic (5:1–9), feeding of the multitude (6:1–14), walking on the water (6:16–21), healing of the man born blind (9:1–7), and the raising of Lazarus (11:1–44). Five narratives describe a believing response to Jesus (2:11; 4:47, 48, 53; 6:2, 5, 14; 9:35, 36, 38; 11:45; 12:10–11). The narrator also mentions the *sēmeia* in summary statements or editorial comments (2:23; 7:5, 31; 12:37).

Galilee and Jerusalem are the settings for believing in Jesus because of his *sēmeia*. At Cana, the changing of water into wine and the healing of the royal official's son have similar features. Both stories indicate an individual who initiates the action and implicitly asks for a miracle, "They have no wine" (2:3); and "he went and begged him to come down and heal his son, for he was at the point of death" (4:47). Jesus, however, rebukes his mother and the royal official: "Woman, what concern is that to you and to me?" (2:4); and "Unless you see signs and wonders you will not believe" (4:48). They repeat their challenge to Jesus: "Do whatever he tells you" (2:25); and "Sir, come down before my little boy dies" (4:49). Jesus maintains the honor of his household and the disciples (2:11), the royal official and his whole household believe in him (4:53).

A third *sēmeion* in Galilee is the feeding of the multitude that follows Jesus because of his signs (6:2). While they believe in him after they were fed abundantly, their enthusiasm urges them to make him a king. Jesus disregards their zeal by departing to the mountain (v. 15).

In Judea, around Jerusalem, there are two healing stories of men whose illnesses isolate them from others. The paralytic and the man born blind are *foil characters* for one another. Jesus' initiative on the Sabbath creates the healings (5:10; 9:16). Each person obeys his order afterward (5:8; 9:7). The healing, however, affects different responses. The paralytic, who is accused of breaking the Sabbath by carrying his mat, defends himself by declaring he is following the orders of the one who healed him (5:9–13). His later encounter with Jesus does not change him. His apparent fear of the authorities and his desire to be disassociated from Jesus prompts him to reveal Jesus' name to those who seek to kill him (5:14–18). In contrast, the former blind man who only knows Jesus' name (9:11) enters into courageous dialogue with the Pharisees twice (9:13–17, 24–34). His personal encounter with Jesus is the climax of believing in him initially (9:35–38).

The raising of Lazarus in Bethany epitomizes Galilean and Judean *sēmeia* with several distinctive differences. In this seventh *sēmeion*, Lazarus' illness is inextricably connected with a manifestation of God's glory, i.e., God's power shines through Jesus' *sēmeion* (11:4). According to the narrator, Jesus' hour of glorification begins, for the raising of Lazarus is the catalyst for plotting Jesus' death (11:45–53). The narrative also draws readers to the drama that precipitates Jesus' passion and death. The basic struggle between life and death is a major focus.

In earlier narratives of healing and feeding in the Book of Signs, Jesus performs a *sēmeion* and speaks about its significance afterward (cf. 5:1–47; 6:1–59; 9:1–41). The literary structure is reversed in the raising of Lazarus where dialogue is prominent about Lazarus' situation and Jesus' self-identification. There is no indication of a miracle until Jesus' command, "Lazarus, come out!" (v. 43).

The characters that appear in John 11 constitute symbolically a full range of responses to Jesus. Readers may identify with one or several characters as the plot unfolds. The unnamed disciples who accompany Jesus play a minor role by misunderstanding what Lazarus' death implies. They can only hear and interpret Jesus' statement literally, "Lord, if he has fallen asleep, he will be all right" (v. 12). Jesus' correction, "Lazarus is dead. . . . Let us go to him" (vv. 14–15), prompts the only named disciple, Thomas, to comment, "Let us also go, that we may die with him" (v. 16). How the disciples accompanied Jesus in the raising of Lazarus and afterwards are left to our imaginations.

Martha's believing in Jesus constitutes a contrast to the disciples. She sends a message with her sister Mary: "Lord, he whom you love is ill" (v. 3). She relies on Jesus, her friend, in this dire situation. Immediately, we are confronted by Jesus' reception of her message. He says to the disciples, "This illness does not lead to death; rather it is for God's glory, so that the Son of God may be glorified through it" (v. 4). The narrator's comment that affirms Jesus' love for Martha, her sister, and Lazarus, appears puzzling when we learn that Jesus "stayed two days longer in the place where he was" (v. 5).

Next, Martha meets Jesus on the road before he even reaches Bethany (vv. 17–20). She wastes no time in greeting her friend. She berates him for his absence; yet, she also expresses confidence in his presence: "But even now I know that God will give you whatever you ask of him" (v. 21). Jesus' reply, "I am the resurrection and the life" (v. 25), prompts Martha to respond with an extraordinary confession, "Yes, Lord, I believe that you are the Messiah, the Son of God, the one coming into the world" (v. 27).

Martha's proclamation parallels Nathanael's, "Rabbi, you are the Son of God! You are the King of Israel!"(1:49). Her statement is a variation of Peter's confession at Caesarea Philippi (Matthew 16:16 par.). It also supersedes the one of the Galilean official. His belief in Jesus' word was followed by the confirming sign that restored life to his son (4:46–53). Martha's belief precedes Jesus' sign and enables her to witness his glory (11:40). Her response is a contrast to the disciples at Cana who saw the sign and then believed in Jesus (2:11).

Martha's final appearance is at the tomb. Here she protests Jesus' request to take away the stone, "Lord, already there is a stench because he has been dead for four days" (v. 39). Some scribes believed that the soul hovered around the dead person's body for three days. After four days, there was no hope. Now, Jesus recalls an earlier conversation with Martha, "Did I not tell you that if you believed, you would see the glory of God?" (v. 41; cf. vv. 4, 23, 25).

Mary is a secondary, two-dimensional character (cf. Luke 10:38–42) when we contrast her with Martha. She does not advance the drama either by her actions or her speech that are stylized to repeat Martha's character and draw attention to her significance (cf. 11:20, 21, 29, 31, 32). Nonetheless, when Jesus sees Mary weeping, "he was greatly disturbed in spirit and deeply moved" (v. 33). The narrator repeats Jesus' agitation as he approaches the tomb (v. 38). Here, it is important to keep in mind the cultural codes of the first century as compared with a postmodern understanding of Jesus' emotional involvement. Jesus was "disturbed" because Mary challenged him publicly. He responded to protect the household of his Father.

Lazarus, their brother, is the only voiceless character in the narrative. His restoration to life essentially links him with Jesus to the extent that the chief priests also plot his death (12:10–11). In chapter 12, his home is the place of hospitality for Jesus. It is where Martha takes on a characteristic role of serving while Mary anoints Jesus' feet (vv. 2–3).

The Judeans also have roles in the narrative. They are generally described in a positive light: consoling Martha and Mary (v. 19), staying with Mary in the house and accompanying her to the grace (v. 31), showing Jesus his friend's tomb (v. 34), and acknowledging Jesus' love for Lazarus (v. 36). After the disagreement over Jesus (vv. 36–37) develops, we notice some changes in them.

The raising of Lazarus elicits faith from one group who was present at the tomb (11:34; 12:11). These persons witness to Jesus because of his *sēmeion* (12:17). The tense of the Greek verb (*emartyrei*) suggests that their faith in Jesus prompts a continuous witness. Some of those present at the tomb, however, report Jesus' action to the authorities (11:46). His sign does not lead to belief. "A great crowd" appears as a third group in chapter 12. Since members of their group are in Jerusalem for the Passover, they are drawn to Jesus because they heard about Lazarus (12:12, 18). Although they greet him enthusiastically with palm branches and acclamation (12:13), there is no indication of subsequent belief.

The religious officials are another group in the narrative (11:46; 12:10, 19). They are generally unnamed like the various groups of "the Jews." The chief priests and Pharisees realize that Jesus' *sēmeia* are dangerously persuasive. "Everyone will believe in him" (11:47–48; cf. 12:11, 19). Caiaphas, the high priest, criticizes and offers them a plan, "You know nothing at all! You do not understand that it is better for you to have one man die for the people than to have the whole nation destroyed" (11:49b–50). His prophecy rallies the officials to plot Jesus' death (v. 53).

How can we evaluate the characters? Lazarus and Martha are the only ones whom Jesus addresses directly. While Lazarus' response to Jesus' command is not recorded, Martha's response is a confession, an appropriate genre of revelation. Jesus identifies himself, "I am (*egō eimi*) the resurrection and the life" (v. 25). He is the life for those "who believe in me, even though they die, will live, and everyone who lives and believes in me will never die" (vv. 25b–26).

Earlier, the narrator notes that believing in Jesus assures that death is not the ultimate condition, "Whoever believes in him should not perish but have eternal life" (3:16b). The death implied in "perish" is clarified in 11:25–26 where physical death is not denied; rather the assurance of everlasting life beyond the grave is emphasized.

Whether or not the noun "life" (zōē) is qualified by the adjective "eternal" (aiōnios) is not significant since whenever "life" appears in any verse of the Gospel, it signifies the life of the Father and Son that is shared by the believer. Participation in divine life is a present reality for the believer.[1]

The witnesses we encounter in the seven narrative scenes of chapter 1 as well as the sēmeia are not the only ones in the Book of Signs. Jesus appeals to the Judeans to believe in his claim for working on the Sabbath by bringing forth witnesses: John the Baptist (5:33–35), his own works (5:36), the Father (5:37–38), and the Scriptures (5:39).

JOHN THE BAPTIST AND HUMAN TESTIMONY

The preparatory witness of John the Baptist is a Johannine motif we noticed earlier in this chapter. His characterization in chapters 1 and 10, whether read historically or symbolically, describes the importance of authentic witness to bring others to believe in Jesus. His proclamation of Jesus' identity (1:19–34) encouraged two of his own disciples to follow Jesus (1:37). Later his witness was confirmed again because it drew others to him (10:41). Although he worked no sēmeion, John's

1. The interpretation of John 11:1–45 appeared earlier in my "Fifth Sunday of Lent, Year A," 533–36.

word was recognized as authentic, "And many believed in him there" (10:42).

The effectiveness of human testimony is not limited historically to Jesus' first disciples. The model of the first disciples' experience continues in the narrative of the Samaritan woman (4:1–42). After the woman's encounter with Jesus (vv. 7–26), her witness becomes a catalyst for the townspeople who believe in him by coming to Jesus (v. 30). In the Book of Glory, too, Jesus' prayer to the Father includes a petition that the disciples will bear witness to him that others may come to believe through their word (17:20). In fact, the entire Gospel is an authentic human witness to bring others to believe in Jesus (19:35; 21:24).

JESUS' WORKS (AND WORDS)

Most verses in the Gospel where we find "works" (*erga*) and "to work" (*ergazomai*) describe the relationship of Jesus' works to the Father. His mission is to accomplish the work of his Father (4:35; 5:36; 17:4). Jesus' obedience to the Father includes his dependency upon him (5:19, 30; 10:25; 14:10). The Hebrew Scriptures describe the Father's work as creating/ sustaining/restoring life as well as the final judgment. Jesus' *sēmeia* continue the Father's work and identify Jesus' works with his Father's (5:17).

To believe in the identity of action and power, however, demands a deeper faith than seeing the *sēmeia* as authenticating Jesus, the wonder worker. It means believing in the relationship of Jesus and the Father because of the *sēmeia*. The indwelling and mutual relationship of Jesus and the Father, however, is revealed only to the disciples. Jesus promises them that they will continue his works (14:10–12).

Jesus' works (*erga*) embrace all that he says and does. What Jesus sees the Father doing, he does (5:19), and what Jesus hears from the Father, he speaks as the basis for his judgment (5:30). The complementary relationship between Jesus' works and word is important. In the Cana healings, belief in Jesus' word is validated by a subsequent sign. In addition, Jesus' word alone is the catalyst for believing in the call of the first disciples, the Samaritans' belief in Jesus (4:42), and the crowd's belief in his word (8:30).

THE FATHER

In addition to the Father's works that Jesus continues through his *sēmeia* (and words) we find another witness (5:32, 36) that Jesus describes to the Judeans:

> And the Father who sent me has himself testified on my behalf. You have never heard his voice or seen his form, and you do not have his word abiding in you, because you do not believe him whom he has sent. (5:37–38)

How is the Father a witness to draw individuals to Jesus? In the Bread of Life discourse, we find three descriptions of the Father's initial role. First, the Father wills all persons to come to Jesus (6:37). Nonetheless, human freedom is not abrogated. An individual decides. Second, the Father draws all persons or gives them to Jesus (6:44–45). Third, the Father gives individuals the capacity or ability to come to Jesus (6:65). The paradox of believing (6:44–45) consists in the Father's drawing of an individual who hears and learns from him; yet, this activity only occurs through Jesus, by whom the Father's words are proclaimed.

THE SCRIPTURES

The term "Scriptures" (*graphē*) appears twelve times in the Gospel. The disciples understand this witness after the resurrection (5:39, 46). The Scriptures also describe the treachery of Judas (13:18; 17:12) as well as how the crucifixion and death of Jesus fulfilled the Scriptures (19:24, 28, 36–37). In addition, there is an extended teaching of Jesus after the feeding of the multitude, the Bread of Life discourse, which interweaves scripture texts with interpretation (6:31–58).

HUMAN FREEDOM

An individual decides personally whether or not to believe in Jesus. In 3:18–21, we see the reasons for choosing and the judgment that results. The indefinite subject "one" emphasizes the function of personal freedom in responding to Jesus' mission of saving the world and not judging it (v. 17). An individual who freely chooses to believe in Jesus is not judged whereas the one who does not believe in him is already judged. The one who believes lives in the light acts accordingly. In contrast, the one who does not believe prefers the darkness and evil works (vv. 19–21).

To believe or not to believe means to take a stance. The one who comes to the light describes the beginning disciple who will continue to practice the truth, whereas the one who chooses to remain in the darkness rejects the light and any relationship to Jesus.

The profound theological insight in these verses lies in the association of a freely chosen decision to believe or not to believe with a self-judgment that determines the individual's present and future direction. While the decision is not limited to a conclusive option, it is expressed in daily life with activity that corresponds to it.[2]

Appropriation: Second Naiveté

Witnesses to Jesus invite readers to believe on the integrity of their word. Would-be disciples, however, need personal experience of Jesus to make an initial commitment to him. The *sēmeia* of Jesus are another witness. Jesus heals, feeds, sustains, and raises up to new life all who encounter him. The narrator does not approve or condemn any catalyst that enables believing in Jesus. The scenes are developed to offer readers connections with personal experience. The dynamism of Jesus' *sēmeia* and teaching, his ability to sustain dialogue with the Samaritan woman and Martha draw some to him. Other readers are intrigued by the conviction of human testimony, the intimacy with the Father and the references to Scripture.

Each of these catalysts requires a decision that is made freely and renewed throughout one's lifetime. Not only is the decision renewable, but also the activities that flow from believing often deepen the believing decision. It is a spiral, a dance, whereby an individual believes and shares the discovery with another. In sharing the discovery, one experiences believing again. Believing does not happen in a vacuum. It occurs through a spiral of dialogue and solitude. Believers intentionally form a community of disciples to share their blessings and to be challenged to believe deeply and broadly.

How do the patterns for becoming God's beloved by making an initial commitment toward believing in Jesus develop in our lives today? Believing in Jesus happens in the

2. Pazdan, *Discipleship*, 119–22, 124, 128–29.

context of relationships. The concept of solitary believers is not a life-giving metaphor for the Johannine community or us. Look back now on the *Reflection Questions: First Naiveté* and your responses. Then review the *Interpretation of the Stories: Critical Inquiry of Christian Tradition*. The process of *Appropriation* happens when there is a connection between the Johannine story and personal living. The connection enables the reader to speak a Johannine story as one's own story. The experiences connect because the same Spirit who inspired the stories is the dynamic link to the stories of our lives.

One way to *appropriate* what you are learning about believing is to enter into theological reflection alone or with others. First, choose a believing story and reflect upon its significance in your life (personal). Next, review the story from the Interpretation (tradition). Then, be attentive for one day to news on the Web, TV, and print media (culture). Is there a connection of the Johannine story to a news event? Reflecting on the relationships of personal experience, Johannine stories and cultural happenings can illumine and stretch your mind and heart.

Another way to *appropriate* what you are learning is to do it contextually. To what situation can you bring your learning? A chat with a neighbor? Speaking with a family member? A professional conversation at work? Reflect on the possibilities and see what happens.

Some persons like to express learning in drawing, painting, movement, playing a musical instrument, writing lyrics or poetry. How could your learning be visualized?

Try some way of *appropriation* before going to the next chapter.

---2---

The Life of Jesus and the Father

Mutual Knowing, Loving, and Abiding

Taking a risk is seldom without some measure of fear. We may take a risk for a better relationship, better employment, or self-improvement. If another person encourages us to take a risk, we often can summon up the courage to do it. Just so, we believe in Jesus as our first commitment toward becoming the beloved of God, we realize that it is an essential wager for the spiritual life of a Christian. In chapter 1, we explored how Jesus' invitation to "come and see" is the catalyst for personal experience (1:35–39) that is often shared with another, e.g., Andrew invites Peter (1:43–44) and Philip invites Nathaniel (1:45–46).

Consequently, what happens to us because we choose to believe in Jesus? We expect change because we risk entering into a new relationship. We know that Jesus' relationship to the Father is his identity. How will this relationship affect us? Will we see and touch and hear differently in our daily lives? Or do we have to wait patiently until after death to share in their life? This chapter invites us to imagine and embrace the mysterious dynamic of mutual life that Jesus shares with the Father.

Reflection Questions: First Naiveté

1. Re-read the prologue of the Gospel, 1:1–18. Write down any words or phrases that describe the relationship of God and the Word. Be attentive, especially, to the verbs. Make a line drawing or a symbol for the relationship of God and the Word.

2. Consider the verb "know." Write down three to five different meanings for the verb. How do these definitions describe the mutual knowing of Jesus and the Father? Recall any stories or teachings of Jesus to illustrate your responses.

3. Consider the verb "love." Write down at least five different meanings for the verb. How do these definitions describe the mutual loving of Jesus and the Father? Recall any stories or teachings of Jesus to illustrate your responses.

4. Consider the verb "abide." Write down at least three different meanings for the verb. How do these definitions describe the mutual abiding of Jesus and the Father? Recall any stories or teachings of Jesus to illustrate your responses.

5. Re-read your responses to 1–4. Do you see any connections between the Prologue and your responses?

Critical Inquiry of Christian Tradition

Jesus and the Father: Mutual Knowing

In the prologue, we hear an astonishing truth that shapes our reading of the entire Gospel: No one has ever seen God. It is God the Father's only Son who lives at the Father's heart who reveals God to us (1:18). In early Christian tradition, Augustine comments that no physical or mental vision has ever embraced God's fullness.[1] Later, Thomas Aquinas agrees that no one has ever seen God, neither with imagination nor with a comprehensive vision. It was "necessary for us to receive wisdom . . . from the competent teacher of wisdom, the Only Begotten Son, *who is in the bosom of the Father*."[2]

For Thomas, "bosom" is "the womb," i.e., "from the inmost secret things of my essence, incomprehensible to every created intellect . . . consubstantial with me and of the same nature and power, and virtue and knowledge."[3] What the Beloved Son reveals surpasses all other teachings because "it was handed on immediately by the Only Begotten Son, who is the first Wisdom."[4]

What does Jesus know (*oida/ginōskō*) about the Father? He knows his personal identity: "I know him because I am from him and he sent me" (7:29), "I know where I have come from and where I am going" (8:14b). Jesus knows whatever he says and does comes from his identity with the Father (3:31–35; 5:19, 30; 12:50b; 17:25). Since Jesus knows the Father completely, he witnesses to the crowd: "I know him;

1. Quoted in St. Thomas Aquinas, *Catena Aurea*, 43.
2. St. Thomas Aquinas *Commentary* 1, §215.
3. Ibid., §217.
4. Ibid., §221.

if I would say that I do not know him, I would be a liar like you. But I do know him and I keep his word" (8:55; cf. 8:18). Likewise, Jesus is confident that the Father witnesses about him: "And the Father who sent me has himself testified on my behalf" (5:37; cf. 5:32).

The Fourth Gospel is a testimony to Jesus' experience of knowing the Father completely. The purpose of Jesus' revelation is "that you may come to believe that Jesus is the Messiah, the Son of God, and that through believing you may have life in his name" (20:31). The author assures hearers and readers of its authenticity. After Jesus' death, we hear, "The one who saw this has testified so that you may also believe. The testimony is true and that one knows that she speaks the truth" (19:35). At the end of the Gospel, listen to a first-person witness, "This is the disciple who is testifying to these things and has written them, and we know that the testimony is true" (21:24). Just as the Beloved Son of the Father who lives at God's heart to reveal God to us (1:18), so, too, the beloved disciple reclines at Jesus' heart to make him known to us (13:23).

The testimony of the Gospel assumes the mutual knowing of Jesus and the Father for its witness and invitation to believe. Jesus declares this reality only once, "Just as the Father knows me and I know the Father" (10:15). The teaching is imbedded in the metaphor of the good shepherd (10:11–15) with whom Jesus identifies: "I am the Good Shepherd" (vv. 11, 14). The "I am" statements are theological metaphors that recall for readers the revelation of God to Moses in the burning bush, "I am who I am" (Exod 3:14; cf. John 6:35; 8:12; 9:5; 10:7, 11, 14; 11:25; 14:6; 15:1).

In vv. 11–15, we notice Jesus' qualifications as the good shepherd. First, his willingness to lay down his life for the sheep is contrasted to the hireling who runs away from them when the wolf comes (vv. 11–12). Second, the mutual knowing of Father and Son expresses the intimacy that motivates Jesus to lay down his life for the sheep (v. 15). Gregory the Great comments that Jesus' love for his sheep shows his love for the Father.[5] Since Jesus knows and loves his Father, he comes not to do his own will but the will of God who sent him (4:34, 5:30, 6:38, 39, 40).[6]

Jesus and the Father: Mutual Loving

In the Prologue we notice that Jesus, the Beloved Son of the Father, lives at God's heart to be God's revelation to us (1:18). What does being at God's heart mean? In the Introduction, I described how cultural anthropologists observe that persons understand one another in Jesus' time by noticing the physical features of others. Each "personality" consists of "zones of interaction," i.e., activities of eyes-heart, ears-mouth, and hands-feet. The activities of the eyes-heart are a zone of emotion-fused thought that includes "sight, insight, understanding, choosing, loving, thinking, valuing . . . ."[7]

Another difference is that in Jesus' time, individuals are not introspective and conscious of themselves as separate persons. Value and honor from others increases as relationships to members of the household are perceived. Every individual is part of a dyadic personality. Jesus, as Son, receives his iden-

5. Quoted in St. Thomas Aquinas, *Catena Aurea*, 354.

6. Howard-Brook, *Becoming Children of God*, 240.

7. Malina and Rohrbaugh, *John*, 35.

tity from his relationship to the Father (and his household). Throughout the Fourth Gospel, Jesus speaks and acts in fidelity to his Father whom he honors and from whom he receives honor. The significance of "honor" is evident in a pericope where Jesus addresses a crowd:

> The Father judges no one but has given all judgment to the Son, so that all may honor the Son just as they honor the Father. Anyone who does not honor the Son does not honor the Father who sent him. (5:23; see 8:49)

What does being at the heart of God mean for Jesus? He experiences not only a mutual relationship of knowing the Father but also a mutual relationship of loving the Father. We realize the integral relationship between knowing and loving when we return to the metaphor of the good shepherd. In v. 17, a theological insight culminates the description of Jesus as the good shepherd, ". . . the Father loves (*agapa*) me, because I lay down my life in order to take it up again." Jesus' freedom is accentuated again in the next verse, "No one takes it from me, but I lay it down of my own accord. I have power to lay it down, and I have power to take it up again. I have received this command from my Father" (v. 18).

The image of "laying down" and "taking up" his life is a memorable description of Jesus' death and resurrection that is theologically distinct from the Synoptic Gospels. Here we see Jesus freely choosing to lay down his life to be glorified by being raised up on the cross. Jesus' authority that is rooted in his Father's command is the catalyst for his actions. In the Johannine passion narrative, Romans and Judeans are secondary characters in Jesus' death.

Aquinas probes v. 17 by asking about the relationship of the Father's love to Jesus' death.[8] Does the Father love Jesus *because* he lays down his life? He offers three possibilities to understand the nuance of the "because" (*hoti*) clause. First, if we interpret the Father's love as the *reason* for Jesus' death, God gives him the effect of love, i.e., glory and exaltation (Phil 2:8). Second, if it indicates an *expression* of love, then the Father decrees that Jesus redeems the human race through his suffering (Rom 8:32). Third, if it is the *sign* of love, then Jesus fulfills his Father's command and endures death. Aquinas prefers the third possibility and notes that the sign of his love excludes the violence of having life snatched from him because he lays down his life voluntarily.[9]

Wes Howard-Brook develops another understanding of the Father's love in v. 17 that may seem "a dissonant note to Christians raised on the idea of God's unconditional love."[10] Neither God's love for Jesus nor his love for the disciples is unconditional because it is "grounded in the willingness of the beloved to witness to their faith by laying down their lives and trusting that they will be received again."[11]

When we examine the second half of the Gospel, the Book of Glory, we find the only verse in the New Testament that explicitly acknowledges Jesus' love for the Father, "so that the world may know that I love the Father" (14:31b). Ordinarily, Jesus' love for the Father is identified with his obedience, "but I do as the Father has commanded me" (14:31a).

---

8. St. Thomas Aquinas *Commentary* 2, §1421.

9. Ibid., §1422.

10. Howard-Brook, *Becoming God's Children*, 241.

11. Ibid.

Just as the mutual knowing of the Father and Jesus in 10:15 is the paradigm for Jesus' love of "his own," so their mutual loving is the model for their love of the disciples. The teaching is embedded in two genres, the image of the vine and branches (15:1–11), and Jesus' prayer (17:1–24) in the Book of Glory. In the first text, we hear another "I am" statement: "I am the (true) vine" (15:1, 5), which is developed in vv. 1–5a. Next, there is the invitation to abide in Jesus (vv. 5b–8). Finally, the model of Jesus and the Father is introduced (vv. 9–11), especially in v. 9a, "As the Father has loved me, so also I have loved you."

The significance of the verbs for "loving" is vigorously debated in classical and Christian philosophy and theology. Often, sharp distinctions are developed between loving friends (*phileō*) and loving God (*agapaō*). In the Gospel of John, however they are interchangeable. In the Book of Signs, the verbs, *agapaō* (3:36; 10:17) and *phileō* (5:20), describe the Father's continuous love for Jesus. In the Book of Glory, however, *agapaō* emphasizes the intensity and depth of the Father's love.

When we analyze the construction in 15:9a, "*As* the Father has loved me, *so* I have loved you," we see that it is more than a comparison. It designates the source and intensity of relationship between Jesus and the disciples. The second part, "so I have loved you," expresses the total self-giving of Jesus in his death and resurrection on behalf of the disciples.

The second text, a part of Jesus' prayer (17:20–24), parallels the first text. As Jesus loves the disciples inasmuch as the Father loves him (15:9a), so the Father loves the disciples as he loves Jesus (17:23b). In these verses, the Father's love for Jesus is the model for their mutual love of the disciples. Similarly, the second construction denotes the source and intensity of the relationship between the Father and the disciples, "*and* I have loved them *even as* you have loved me."

Jesus and the Father: Mutual Abiding

In the early christological hymn of the prologue, we notice the foundation of the mutual knowing and loving paradigm (v. 18). Here we also locate the third mutual relationship, "abiding." Verse 1 declares that the Word was in God's presence, i.e., in a dynamic sense of accompanying God. Verse 18 echoes the reality of the Beloved Son being at the heart of God. Frank Moloney translates both verses to emphasize that as the Word is turned toward God (1:1) now Jesus is turned toward the Father (1:18) throughout the narrative of the Gospel.[12]

In the Last Supper Discourses (chaps. 14–17), the verb "being" (*einai*) and a prepositional phrase describes Jesus' indwelling with the Father, "I am in my Father" (14:10). The same structure of verb and prepositional phrase states their mutual relationship, "I am in the Father and the Father is in me" (14:11). Jesus' prayer to the Father also witnesses to their relationship, "as you, Father, are in me and I am in you" (17:21).

The verb "abiding" (*menō*) with a prepositional phrase is a distinctive Johannine construction that expresses a permanent, mutual relationship between Jesus and the Father. In 15:10, Jesus declares to the disciples, "I have kept my Father's commandments and abide in his love."

12. Moloney, *Gospel of John*, 33, 46–47.

Relationships between Mutual
Knowing, Loving, and Abiding

What the prologue proclaims about the mutual relationship of Jesus and the Father, the Gospel affirms in Jesus' teaching, his identity as the good shepherd, and his prayer to the Father. I consider the relationships separately, but they are simultaneous and inseparable since they describe the mutual life of Jesus and the Father. It is interesting that the relationships are explicit in the Gospel but are not developed at length. Rather, they constitute an invitation to readers to consider the possibilities of sharing in the mutual life of Jesus and the Father. In addition, the relationships that extend to believers are developed with greater detail. These texts are interpreted in the next chapter.

Appropriation: Second Naiveté

Just as believing in Jesus takes place in the context of relationships, so the life of Jesus and the Father is constituted by mutual relationships. The challenge in this chapter is reflection upon the experience that Jesus and the Father share in their mutual knowing, loving, and abiding. Look back now on the *Reflection Questions: First Naiveté* and your responses. Then review *Interpretation of the Stories: Critical Inquiry of Christian Tradition*. What new connections do you see? Write them down.

Next, visualize the mutual relationships of the Father and Jesus by an abstract or concrete sketch with some colored markers. You may wish to go to a daily newspaper and some magazines. Cut out words and pictures that represent their relationships. Add them to your drawing or put them on a separate sheet of paper. The drawing and the design offer you a clue about what you treasure in these relationships.

Share your connections about the chapter and the drawing with one other person or in a small group. What do the connections and drawings say about your life? Do others have similar experiences? How does media news confirm or contradict your shared experiences?

Another way to appropriate what you are learning is to do it contextually. To what situation can you bring your learning? A chat with a neighbor? Speaking with a family member? A professional conversation at work? Reflect on the possibilities and see what happens.

The Life of God's Beloved

*Mutual Knowing, Loving,
and Abiding in God's Household*

What happens when we believe in Jesus? Although the Gospel of John is sometimes interpreted as a "Jesus and me" spirituality, the label is inadequate. On the one hand, as disciples of Jesus, we become God's beloved and our relationships with God, Jesus, and one another change and develop. Relating to Jesus and the Father in a life of mutual knowing, loving, and abiding is a great mystery that we can appropriate only by believing and living in the mystery one day at a time. On the other hand, our daily relationships with one another are concrete manifestations of our relationships with Jesus and the Father.

We nourish our spiritual lives with prayer and meditation. These practices often give energy and wisdom to our lives. Without being in relationships, however, there is no spiritual life. All relationships have the possibility of being encounters, i.e., touching and embracing *life*, with others, Jesus, and God. Relationships with family members, friends, co-workers, persons who enter our lives for a moment or a day, are the locus for vigorous spiritual lives. In this chapter we interpret the dynamic relationships as disciples with Jesus and the Father. We also reflect on how these relationships affect our lives in God's household with others who are God's beloved.

Reflection Questions

1. Think about on your experience of being an individual with particular gifts and limitations. How do you know them? Who tells you?

2. On a sheet of paper make three columns to describe gifts, limitations, and persons or situations that offer you self-knowledge.

3. Reflect on how you know you are a gifted and limited person from your experiences of Jesus and the Father.

4. On a second sheet of paper, label the three columns, gifts, limitations, and experiences of Jesus and the Father. Fill in the columns.

5. Go back to your *Reflection Questions* for chapter 2. Re-read questions and responses to 2–4. Compare them to what you have written down for this chapter. What happens? Can you make a drawing or a symbol with colored pencils to express your experience?

Critical Inquiry of Christian Tradition

Mutual Knowing: Jesus, the Father and the Beloved

Eternal life, sharing in the life of God, happens when individuals choose to believe in Jesus. Being disciples is a commitment to sustained believing. In contrast, those who do not believe do not choose to share life with Jesus. Some individuals are not convinced by Jesus' *sēmeia*, witnesses, works and words, the Father, and the Scriptures to make a personal, free decision to believe (chapter 1). The distinction between disciples and non-disciples (*foil characters*) is evident when we consider what the Gospel offers us about "knowing."

The disciples who follow Jesus desire a relationship with him (chapter 1). In the first *sēmeion,* changing water into wine (2:1–11), the disciples are singled out as those who believe in him because Jesus reveals his glory (2:11). "Glory" (*doxa*) may be a memory of the Johannine community of how God was present to the Hebrew people in their journey through the wilderness. They knew God's presence in a cloud and a pillar of fire. They knew God did not abandon them because they were provided with water, manna and quail (Exod 16–17). "Glory" may also refer to another memory of Moses' encounter with God when he entered the Tent of Meeting while the people stayed outside. In that holy place the Lord would speak to Moses "face to face as one speaks to a friend" (Exod 33:11).

The disciples will know Jesus after his hour of glory, too. Jesus' hour (*kairos*) is the crucifixion event when he departed from the disciples to go back to the Father (John 13:1). After the resurrection the disciples will know Jesus and the Father anew.

For the foil characters, however, knowing Jesus is of little consequence because they do not desire any relationship with him. Their knowledge is based on their own presumptions, not on what he may reveal about himself.

Knowing Jesus' identity, especially his origin, is a common interest for the disciples and the foil characters. The question of origin is essential since Jesus' identity is based on his relationship to God as beloved son. The Judeans deny Jesus' heavenly origins (6:42) and affirm his earthly origin (7:27). Jesus, in turn, responds variously to the foil characters' assumptions. He orders them to stop complaining about his teaching (6:43) and reveals that believing in him is the basis for knowing his origin (6:44–46).

We can compare some differences between the foil characters and the disciples when we analyze 8:14–21 and 14:2–9. Please pause to read these passages now. Both the Pharisees and Thomas do not know (*oida*) Jesus' origin or his return to the Father (8:14; 14:5). Thomas alone receives Jesus' revelation that he provides access to the Father (14:6). Again, while the Pharisees and Philip do not know the Father (8:19; 14:8), the latter receives the revelation that seeing Jesus is seeing the Father (14:9). While the Judeans know neither Jesus nor the Father, Jesus confirms that the incomplete but genuine knowing of him and the Father belongs to the disciples (14:7).

Contrasting Models of Knowing and Believing (3:1–21 and 4:1–42)

Jesus' dialogue with Nicodemus (3:1–21) and a woman of Samaria (4:1–42) is an invitation to know him by believing in what he says. See chart 3.1, **Knowing and Being Known**, to locate the narrative characters. There are striking differences between the characters that Jesus encounters to draw us into

CHART 3.1
Knowing and Being Known—Narrative Scenes: 3:1–21 and 4:1–42

Nicodemus: 3:1–21		A Woman of Samaria: 4:1–42
		Transitional Scene. 4:1–4.
	SETTING	Judea to Galilee via Samaria (v. 3)
	CHARACTERS	"Jesus" (v. 1)
	CONFLICT	What will Jesus do when he hears a comparison of his and John's baptizing disciples through the active gossip network?[a] (vv. 1–2)
	DENOUEMENT	Jesus decides to return to Galilee via Samaria (vv. 3–4).
Scene One. 3:1–10.		**Scene One. 4:5–15.**
Jerusalem implied (See 2:23), night (v. 2)	*SETTING*	A Samaritan city "Sychar near plot that Jacob had given Joseph," his well, at noon (vv. 5–6)
	CHARACTERS	*Jesus* (vv. 6, 10, 13) *a Jew* (v. 9) *Sir* (v. 11,15)
A Pharisee (v. 1) named *Nicodemus* (vv. 1, 4, 9) *a leader of the Jews* (v. 1) *a teacher of Israel* (v. 10)		*a Samaritan woman* (v. 7) the *Samaritan woman* (v. 9) the *woman* (vv. 11, 15)
Jesus *Rabbi . . . teacher who has come from God* no one can do these **signs** that you do apart from the **presence of God** (v. 2; cf.1:2)		

Identity in an honor-shame culture is a complex status in a highly structured world of boundaries to determine holiness (purity). Religious groups: Pharisees, lay scholars, who interpreted the Torah and oral tradition to enable persons to live a life pleasing to God. Cf. Sadducees, Essenes and Zealots. Social unity includes economic status and geographical location. "Authentic" Jews lived in Jerusalem. Cf. Galilee and Samaria. Holiness includes adherence to strict gender roles and behavior.

Note: This chart is a visual tool for understanding the drama of Jesus, Nicodemus, and the Woman of Samaria according to the narrative scenes of chapters 3 and 4. The italicized words signify narrative components and the characters. The bold words indicate theological terms that are important throughout the Gospel.

[a] Gossip is oral information about public persons whom individuals may have witnessed in public. Sometimes the gossip includes an evaluation of the honor-shame situation.

Scene One. 3:1–10 (continued)	CONFLICTS	Scene One. 4:7–15 (continued).
How will Nicodemus and Jesus interact with one another? Is genuine dialogue for challenge-riposte[b] probable? What are significant narrative and symbolic clues in the scene that would alert hearers and readers?	Irony and misunderstanding alert hearers and readers about how to evaluate conflict. Irony occurs when a character perceives one level of meaning and the other intends another level whereas misunderstanding occurs when a character interprets another on a literal level. **Punning,** a play on words, adds subtlety to dialogue.	How will a woman of Samaria interact with Jesus? Is genuine dialogue for challenge-riposte probable? What are significant narrative and symbolic clues in the scene that would alert hearers and readers?
Nicodemus comes to Jesus at **night. We know** this signals Jesus' credibility (v. 2). As a *literalist,* however, Nicodemus cannot imagine another possibility of **being born from above/ born again, or born of water and the Spirit** (vv. 3–8). He dismisses Jesus' teaching with a put-down (v. 9). Jesus responds with a negative challenge (v. 10).	DENOUEMENT	*Jesus and the woman* **invert purity codes** by speaking to one another. She **knows** her tradition and **challenges** Jesus about their people's mutually hostile relationship (v. 9) and the well (vv. 11–12). The woman misunderstands Jesus' teaching about a **spring of water gushing up to eternal life** (vv. 13–14). She requests **water** to satisfy her thirst and cancel the necessity of drawing water (v. 15).
Scene Two. 3:11–21. Same	SETTING	**Scene Two. 4:16–26. Scene Two. 4:16–26** Same
Same	CHARACTERS	Same
What does monologue replacing dialogue signify? Who listens to the new teaching?	CONFLICTS	What will happen in the dialogue?

[b] Challenge-riposte is a public, social communication about honor. The communication is always conducted by equals. It is characterized by a stereotypical sequence. A male offers a challenge (word, gesture, or action) to another male who perceives it and responds. A challenge can be positive (praise, a gift) as well as negative (an insult, a threat). An audience evaluates the reaction of the one who is challenged.

Scene Two. 3:11-21 (continued)	DENOUEMENT	Scene Two. 4:16-26 (continued)
The *characters* **testify** about what they **know** and **have seen.** They challenge *Nicodemus* to **believe** their heavenly teaching (vv. 11–13). *Jesus, the Son of Man,* has come down from heaven and will return by being **lifted up.** The spatial metaphor describes *Jesus'* **crucifixion and return to the Father** that give **eternal life** to everyone who **believes** (vv. 14–15). *Jesus,* God's only Son, is sent to **save the world** (vv. 16–17). Anyone who **does not believe in Jesus,** the only Son of God, **is already condemned** (v. 18). The *individual,* who prefers **darkness to light,** engages in evil activities (vv. 19–20). Anyone who **believes in Jesus is not condemned.** The *individual* lives the truth by **acting in the light** with deeds clearly rooted in God (v. 21).		*Jesus* **knows** the woman's story, **challenges** her and she responds truthfully (vv.16–18). She sees him as **prophet** and **challenges** him about her tradition of **worship** (vv. 19–20). *Jesus* responds: **True worship of God is in spirit and truth** (v. 24). Again the woman challenges *Jesus* about the coming **Messiah.** *Jesus* responds: **I am he** (vv. 25–26). **Scene Three. 4:27.** *SETTING.* Same *CHARACTERS. Jesus, the woman, the disciples.* *CONFLICT.* Why do the disciples say nothing to *Jesus* about speaking to a woman? *DENOUEMENT.* Unresolved conflict. **Scene Four. 4:28–30.** *SETTING.* Sychar *CHARACTERS.* the *woman* and *people of Sychar* *CONFLICT.* Will the townspeople **believe the woman's testimony**: **Come and see** a man who told me everything I have ever done! He cannot be the *Messiah,* can he? (v. 29). *DENOUEMENT. Townspeople* leave and **go to meet** *Jesus.* **Scene Five. 4:31-38.** *SETTING.* Outside Sychar *CHARACTERS. Jesus and disciples* *CONFLICT.* Will the disciples understand *Jesus'* teaching? *DENOUEMENT. Jesus'* monologue does not resolve the conflict. **Scene Six. 4:39-42.** *SETTING.* Outside Sychar *CHARACTERS. Jesus and townspeople* *CONFLICT.* Will *Jesus* **receive** *Samaritans* who **came** to him? Will he accept their invitation to **remain** with them? *DENOUEMENT. Townspeople* **believed in** *Jesus* because the *woman* **testified.** *Jesus* **remained** with them and **his word** (vv. 40-41). Then *townspeople* addressed the *woman*: We have heard for ourselves, we **know** that this is **truly the Savior**

the power of his words and human responses. Please pause to read John 3 and 4 before continuing.

The stories dramatize the absolute contrasts between honor and shame codes that were prevalent in Jesus' day. First, the settings symbolize purity and pollution. Jerusalem (3:2) is holy since the second temple and its officials reside there. In contrast, the Samaritan city of Sychar (4:5) is sinful according to the Judeans of Jerusalem because its people traced their lineage to the kingdom of Israel. The people were considered unclean due to intermarrying, building a rival temple to Jerusalem, and not sending contributions its temple.

Second, the individuals are described according to honor and shame labels. Nicodemus has all the status names of prestige and privilege, "A *Pharisee* . . . a *leader* of the Judeans . . . a *teacher* of Israel" (3:1, 10). In contrast, a woman of Samaria embodies apparent exclusion from any honor and acceptance. The "woman" is described four times according to regional identification, "Samaritan" (4:7–10), and her status is unacceptable, "Judeans do not share things in common with *Samaritans*" (4:9).

Third, when we read the dialogues between Jesus and the characters, they are marvelous examples of challenge-riposte (see introduction, under A Challenging Gospel) as well as distinctive development. In the Mediterranean world of Jesus, daily living for males included outwitting one another in conversations, whereas women did not speak in the public arena. The honor of one's household was at stake in the dialogue. Honor could be attributed to one's status at birth (ascribed honor) as well as what happens in conversations (acquired honor). Sometimes the interchange was positive in giving the other a compliment. At other times, it was a negative to challenge the honor of the individual and his household.

Nicodemus begins his conversation by complementing Jesus, "a *teacher* who has *come from God*; for no one can do these *signs* (*sēmeia*) that you do apart from the presence of God (3:2). Notice Jesus pays no attention to the flattery by introducing another thought entirely. He challenges Nicodemus' theology by the necessity of being "born from above" in order to "see the kingdom of God" (v. 3). Nicodemus misunderstands Jesus by taking in his words literally and conjuring up the image of returning to a mother's womb as an old man (v. 4).

However, Jesus counters by equating "water" and "Spirit" with "begotten from above" (vv. 5–8). When Nicodemus asks how it will happen, Jesus responds rhetorically, "You hold the office of teacher of Israel and still you do not understand these matters?" (vv. 9–10). The narrator does not record Nicodemus' response, and he is shamed because he does not respond. There is no additional dialogue to Jesus' invitation to know the truth. Later, Nicodemus' status is changed by the way he relates to the chief priests and Pharisees (7:45–52) and Joseph of Aramathea (19:38–42).

It is quite a different situation when Jesus begins a dialogue with the woman of Samaria. He speaks to a woman who is both without "ascribed" honor and possible "acquired" honor. His challenge begins lively dialogue (4:7). In her role as *teacher*, she questions his demand for water, "You are a Judean. How can you ask me, a Samaritan and a woman, for a drink?" (v. 9). His statement challenges her imagination, "If only you recognized God's gift, and who it is that is asking you for a drink, you would have asked him instead, and he would have given you living water" (v. 10).

Instead of asking how this will happen as Nicodemus inquired earlier, the woman reveals her own logic. Without a bucket to draw from the deep well, how will Jesus produce the "living water"? (v. 11a). Again as a *teacher*, she recalls her own history about Jacob and the well. Ironically, she dismisses Jesus' greater claims with another question (vv. 11b–12). Jesus declares that his gift of water will satiate a person's thirst definitively. How? It will become "a spring of water gushing up to eternal life" (v. 14).

The woman does not resist Jesus now. Not to be thirsty and no more daily trips to draw water from the well are wonderful possibilities in her life: "Sir, give me this water," she exclaims (v. 15). Next, she listens to Jesus who commands her to call her husband and return to him (v. 16). The woman's reply, however, is a subtle change from the first scene where she was instructing Jesus with well-known tradition. Here she speaks the truth of her present situation: "I have no husband" (v. 17a). By acknowledging her past and present situation, Jesus enables the woman to create his new identity. She calls him a "prophet" and refers to the tradition of different locales of worship for Samaritans and Judeans (vv. 19–20). Jesus knows her life, and she recognizes him anew.

The woman's understanding of "prophet" leads to Jesus' instruction on worship (vv. 21–24). Now she connects the function of prophet to the coming Messiah (v. 25). Jesus again acknowledges the truth of her statement: "I who speak to you am he" (*egō eimi*, v. 26). Unlike Nicodemus, however, the woman leaves Jesus to acknowledge her experience to the townspeople. She imagines the possibility of Jesus as the Messiah (vv. 28–29). The effect of her knowing Jesus and witnessing prompts them to come to Jesus (v. 30).

Finally, the scene shifts to the townspeople. They are believers in Jesus through the catalyst of the woman's proclamation. After asking Jesus to spend time with them, their belief deepens through Jesus' word. They can witness to him with an extraordinary claim: "we know that this truly is the Savior of the world" (vv. 39–42).

The narrator neither praises nor condemns Nicodemus' model of initial discipleship nor the woman's mature discipleship. As readers we can assume either model for ourselves and ponder personally the relationship of "believing."

Mutual Knowing: Jesus and the Disciples

Another point of view on "knowing" Jesus develops from chapter 2 where we noticed the identification of Jesus as the Good Shepherd (10:11–18). In the center of these verses, Jesus declares, "I know my own and my own know me, just as the Father knows me and I know the Father" (10:14b–15b). The phrase "my own" (*ta ema*) occurs twice, as well, to modify the "sheep" (*probata*) in vv. 26 and 27. Later, when Jesus prays to the Father, he declares, "All mine (*ta ema*) are yours and yours are mine (*ta ema*)" (17:10). In the Prologue we hear, "He came to what was his own (or his own home) and his own did not receive him" (1:11).

What is necessary to become one of Jesus' own? In the beginning of chapter 10, we see that Jesus, the Good Shepherd, calls his sheep by name. They recognize his voice and follow him (10:3b–5). Jesus claims the sheep, and they respond. This mutual pattern of knowing and responding is evident in several post-resurrection narratives that are discussed in chapter 4. See chart 3.2, **The Life of God's Beloved**.

What happens to the disciples when they "know" Jesus? Personal freedom is one gift. Please pause to read John 8:31–36. Jesus addresses Judeans who believed in him with a challenge. Being disciples means being really free (vv. 31, 36). When Jesus equates freedom as knowing the truth, i.e., remaining in his word, the crowd bristles, denies slavery as children of Abraham, and asks him for an explanation (vv. 32–33).

Jesus replies by identifying the slave as the one who acts sinfully whereas the son "has a place forever" (vv. 34–35). Freedom is release *from* sin *for* kinship with God. Only Jesus can truly free the one who believes in him because he is the beloved son of the Father (v. 36). A disciple shares in Jesus' sonship as a member of God's household. In addition, being a disciple means being free *from* servitude and *for* friendship with Jesus (15:12–17).

How does "knowing" affect members of God's household? Individuals who are attentive to being mutually known by Jesus and the Father are open to the possibility of genuinely knowing one another. In chapter 1, we observed how individuals who followed Jesus experienced him by spending time with him (1:37–39). They shared their new understanding with a family member (1:40–42) as well as others (1:45–50). The woman of Samaria, too, spent time with Jesus in lively dialogue before she went back to her people. Being a witness to others is a continuous activity within God's household that encourages openness, listening, questioning, and responding. Disciples witness their experience of Jesus and the Father to

CHART 3.2

The Life of God's Beloved:
Mutual Knowing, Loving, and Abiding in God's Household
The Model of Mutual Relationships: Jesus and the Father

Model: John 10:14–15 I am the good shepherd. I know my own and my own know me just as the Father knows me and I know the Father. **Invitation: Mutual knowing (John 3:1–21, 4:1–42).** Jesus challenges *Nicodemus* to risk entering into dialogue with him for an experiential relationship. *Nicodemus* prefers to **know about** him (3:2). Jesus also challenges *a woman of Samaria* to experience mutual **knowing**. She risks dialogue and personal disclosure. She gains insight about Jesus. She **shares her experience** with townspeople who become believers, too.	**Model: John 15:9a** As the Father has loved me, so I have loved you. **John 17:23b** (you) have loved them even as you have loved me. **Invitation: Mutual loving (John 15:12–17).** Jesus challenges the *disciples*: This is my commandment, that you **love one another as I have loved you** (v. 12). No one has greater love than this, to lay down one's life for one's friends (v. 13). **Mutual friendship** is for others: "And I appointed you **to go and bear fruit**, fruit that will last" (v. 16b).	**Model: John 14:11** I am in the Father and the Father is in me. **John 17:21** As you, Father, are in me and I am in you, may they also be in us. **Invitation: Mutual abiding (John 15:1–8).** Jesus challenges the *disciples*: I am **the vine, you are the branches** (v. 5). **Abide in me as I abide in you.** As the branch cannot bear **fruit** from itself unless it **abides** on the vine, neither can you unless you **abide in me** (v. 4). **Mutual abiding** is for others: **Bear much fruit and become my disciples** (v. 8).

Note: This chart is a visual tool for understanding the life of God's beloved in God's household. The mutual relationships between Jesus and the Father (chapter 2) are outlined in the first half of the chart. The invitations to disciples to experience the Jesus–Father relationships as beloved in God's household (chapter 3) are outlined in the second half of the chart. The bold words indicate theological terms that are important throughout the Gospel. The italicized words refer to the addressees of Jesus' words.

others. Knowing another can be a blessing of knowing Jesus and the Father, too.

Mutual Loving: Jesus, the Father, and the Beloved

Sharing in the life of Jesus and the Father is also an experience of being loved. In the Gospel, we find many insights about loving to understand our relationships to Jesus, the Father, and one another. In the Book of Signs, the narrator describes Jesus' love for Martha, Mary, and Lazarus (11:5), as well as his particular love for Lazarus (11:3, 11, 36). In the Book of Glory, we find the appearance of the Beloved Disciple, "the one whom Jesus loved," (13:23; 19:26; 20:2; and 21:7, 20, 24) as well as Jesus' love for the disciples (13:1, 33, 34; 14:21; 15:9, 12).

Jesus also speaks to the foil characters, "If God were your Father, you would love (*ēgapate*) me, for I came from God and now I am here" (8:42). The verse states a contrary-to-fact relationship. Indeed, the narrator links them with specific attitudes toward Jesus, namely, "hating" (5:18, 19, 23–24), "killing" (5:18; 7:1, 19, 20, 25; 8:37, 40; 11:53; 18:31), and "persecuting" him (5:16; 16:20). Since there is a conscious refusal to believe, there is no love of Jesus, the Father, and the beloved in the household of God. Then, who or what is loved? Preferred?

One choice is the love of darkness. "And this is the judgment, that the light has come into the world, and people loved darkness (*skotos*) rather than light (*phōs*) because their deeds were evil" (3:19). Again, "For all who do evil hate the light and do not come to the light so that their deeds may not be exposed" (v. 20). In contrast, "But those who do what is true come to the light, so that it may be clearly seen that their deeds have been done in God" (v. 21).

To remain here is to freely choose to be without God. It is loving what one possesses or what one is apart from God and without God. It is a preference for one's own evil works rather than a willingness to accept any relationship with Jesus, the light.[1]

The second preference is the love of human glory that keeps some of the authorities from professing their belief in Jesus (12:43). It is preference for false greatness that is enjoyed apart from God. The individual cannot accept God who is offered through Jesus.[2]

The third favorite is love for one's one life (12:25). It is the culpable love that is condemned because it implies an inordinate self-love in preference to loving Jesus. The opposition of self-loving to believing is apparent (although not explicit) because self-love leads to the loss of eternal life, while believing leads to a participation in it.[3]

The fourth love is the love of the world and its manifestations (1 John 2:15–16) that is opposed to believing because these loves are not "from the father." Here "world" is not synonymous with non-believers. Rather, it designates those irreconcilable forces that prevent a true love of the Father. Verse 16 defines them as self-satisfaction (desire of the flesh and eyes) and self-exaltation (pride in riches). They are components of self-love, which seeks its own good and deliberately avoids any relationship with God.

1. Barrosse, "The Relationship of Love to Faith in St. John," 545–47.
2. Ibid., 549.
3. Ibid., 550.

The foil characters that were introduced in chapter 1 can be read as consistent literary devices throughout the Gospel. However, these characters can also be read theologically. As disciples we can put on the personality and attitudes of the foil characters to assess whether or not our living mirrors "believing" in Jesus. We can reflect on whether or not our "knowing" Jesus is based on personal assumptions rather than a willingness to know him experientially. The "loving" preferences of the foil characters may be our occasional or characteristic attitudes, too.

Mutual Love of Jesus, the Father, and the Beloved: A Model of Friendship

How can we imagine the mutual love that unites Jesus, the Father, and the beloved in God's household? Please refer to the chart above, **The Life of God's Beloved**. We direct our focus by returning to the vine and branches pericope (15:1–11). In chapter 2, we discovered, "*As* the Father has loved me, *so* I have loved you" (v. 9a). Now we consider the depth of Jesus' love for the beloved.

Jesus' teaching on friendship (15:12–17) is extraordinary in its weaving together of Jesus' love for the disciples and his invitation for them to love members of God's household. Thomas Aquinas offers us amazing insight about this teaching when Jesus declares to the disciples during their meal in the Upper Room, "No one has greater love than this, to lay down one's life for one's friends" (v. 13). He asserts that Christ laid down his life for his enemies "to make him his friends."[4]

---

4. Thomas Aquinas *Commentary* 2, §2009.

Thomas also states that laying down one's life for one's friends is the sign of the greatest love "because there are four lovable things to put in order: God, our soul, our neighbor, and our body. We should love God more than ourselves and our neighbor, so that for the sake of God we ought to give ourselves, body and soul, for our neighbor."[5]

Jesus continues, "You are my friends if you do what I command you" (v. 14). For Thomas, "friends" can be understood in two ways, namely, either because one loves or one is loved. Similarly, "if you do what I command you," means that a friend, who is a guardian of one's soul, will guard or keep God's commandments. Also, God confers grace and helps those who are loved to keep the commandments. "It is not they who first loved God, but God makes them lovers by loving them."[6]

The sign of Christ's friendship is the heart of v. 15, "I do not call you servants any longer, because the servant does not know what the master is doing; but I have called you friends, because I have made known to you everything that I have heard from my Father." Thomas comments: "a friend reveals the secrets of his heart to his friend . . . Now God reveals his secrets to us by letting us share in his wisdom: 'In every generation she [Wisdom] passes into holy souls and makes them friends of God and prophets' (Wis 7:27)."[7] Catherine of Siena observes, "secrets are shared only with a friend who has become one with oneself."[8]

---

5. Ibid.
6. Ibid., §2011.
7. Ibid., §2016.
8. Catherine of Siena *The Dialogue* no. 60, 115.

What does Jesus hear from the Father? Correspondingly, what do the disciples hear from Jesus? For Thomas, Jesus hears the knowledge of his essence from the Father that he shares with his disciples.[9] Gregory the Great comments,

> All the things he has made known to his servants are the joys of interior love and the feasts of our heavenly fatherland, which he excites in our minds every day by the breath of his love. For as long as we love the sublime heavenly things we have heard, we already know what we love, because the love itself is knowledge.[10]

As a contemporary interpreter, I interpret John 15:15 within the theology of the Fourth Gospel. Jesus—whose life with the Father includes dynamic, mutual knowing—shares that reality with the disciples and invites them to share in their life.[11]

The cause of friendship is described in v. 16a, "You did not choose me but I chose you." Thomas comments,

> It is the usual practice for each one of us to say that he or she is the cause of friendship. . . . Our Lord rejects this . . . He [says]: Whoever has been called to this sublime friendship should not attribute the cause of this friendship to himself, but to me, who chose him or her as a friend . . . . So, I have chosen you by predestining you from all eternity, and by calling you to the faith during your lifetime.[12]

---

9. St. Thomas Aquinas *Commentary* 2, §2017.

10. Ibid., §2018.

11. Pazdan, *Discipleship*, 311–13; idem, "Gifts, Challenges, and Promises," 78.

12. St. Thomas Aquinas *Commentary* 2, §§2019, 2024.

Being chosen for friendship with Jesus is just the beginning. In v. 16b, Jesus continues, "And I appointed you to go and bear fruit, fruit that will last, so that the Father will give you whatever you ask in my name." For Thomas, the verse implies going to travel "over the whole world to convert the whole world to the faith . . . [which] is the fruit of conversion . . . so that the faithful would be led into eternal life and their spiritual fruit flourish."[13]

How do we as beloved in God's household respond to the love of Jesus and the Father? We savor the beauty of friendship that is offered to us. We remember how Jesus identifies himself with the Good Shepherd who freely lays down his life for his sheep (10:14). Jesus' teaching frames the friendship imagery, "This is my command, that you love one another as I have loved you" (15:12, 17). He introduces the command earlier at the supper:

> I give you a new commandment, that you love one another. Just as I have loved you, you also should love one another. By this everyone will know that you are my disciples, if you have love for one another. (13:34–35)

How can we understand "loving one another"? In the Gospel, "one another" (*allēlous*) designates the disciples. Their believing in Jesus separates them from the world, constitutes them as sisters and brothers of Jesus, and offers them God as Father (20:17). It is the mutual love of the disciples that is a participation in the mutual love of Father and Son as well

13. Ibid., §2027. Thomas Aquinas' interpretation of John 15:12–17 appeared earlier in my "Thomas Aquinas and Contemporary Biblical Interpreters," 473–74.

as in the love of the Father and Son for the disciples. These relationships exist only among believers.[14]

Are the "outsiders," the foil characters, excluded? There is no explicit statement in the Gospel. The love of the disciples for one another is emphasized in the Farewell Discourses (chaps. 13–17) where there is a particular focus and urgency to express the command of mutual love as *the* characteristic that defines the disciples. We cannot conclude, however, that the explicit limit of love is also an exclusive one since the love of the Father and Jesus is not limited to believers.[15]

Mutual Abiding: Jesus, the Father, and the Beloved

We return to chapter 15 to understand how Jesus, the Father, and the beloved of God's household abide in one another. Please refer to chart above, The Life of God's Beloved. Then, pause to read 15:1–11. First, notice the close relationship between Jesus, "I am the true vine," and the Father, "my Father is the vine grower" (v. 1). The Father cultivates and prunes the vine for fruitfulness (v. 2).

Thomas Aquinas describes "cultivation":

> Now to cultivate something is to devote one's interest to it. And we can cultivate something in two ways: either to make what is cultivated better, as we cultivate a field . . . or to make ourselves better by the cultivating, and in this way we cultivate wisdom. God cultivates us to make us better by his work, since he roots out the evil seeds in our hearts . . . . But we cultivate God . . . by adoring, in order that we may be made better by him: 'If any one is

14. Lazure, *Les Valeurs morales,* 232.
15. Schnackenburg, *Gospel of John,* 3:55.

a worshiper,' that is, a cultivator of God, 'and does
his will, God listens to him' (9:31).[16]

Next, Jesus offers a precept to the disciples, "Abide in me
as I abide in you. Just as the branch cannot bear fruit by itself
unless it abides in the vine, neither can you unless you abide
in me" (vv. 4–5). Thomas enumerates how abiding in Jesus
brings forth fruit in this life. It enables us to: a) avoid sin, b)
be eager to accomplish works of holiness, c) be eager for the
progress of others, d) enjoy eternal life.[17] Jesus also describes
the effect of not abiding in him, "(be) thrown away like a
branch and withers; such branches are gathered, thrown into
the fire and burned" (v. 6).

What does "mutual abiding" mean? "To abide" (*menō*)
suggests "a deeply personal and constant union."[18] It is a mutual presence of reciprocal knowing and loving. For Henri
Nouwen, cultivating presence is one way of claiming our
status as beloved of God.[19] Mutual presence implies a sharing
with one another rather than a dependency of one *upon* the
other. Mutual abiding is the basic relationship from whose
fountain mutual knowing and loving spring forth and over-
flow (4:14; 7:38).

The abiding relationship expresses essential, personal
relationships. It does not exist for itself as a type of mystical
union that is available to a few persons.[20] Rather, the beloved
enjoys a personal community of life with God by believing

16. St. Thomas Aquinas *Commentary* 2, §1982.

17. Ibid., §1992.

18. Dumm, *Mystical Portrait*, 58.

19. Nouwen, *Life of the Beloved*, 64.

20. McPolin, "Johannine Mysticism," 35. See Brown, *John*, 1:512.

in Jesus. Mutual knowing and loving are the consequences of believing in him. These experiences do not exist in a vacuum. They involve a radical transformation of life because the disciple shares these experiences with believers and foil characters alike.

Mutual abiding is revelation for others. Disciples reveal God's glory in their daily lives. The divine glory that was expressed in Jesus continues in the life of the Church.[21] This "glory" is inextricably linked to "bearing much fruit" (15:8) not only within the community of believers, but also in going outside the community to continue Jesus' word and works in the world. The gift of Jesus after his resurrection enables the disciples' mission, "'*As* the Father has sent me, *so* I send you.' . . . he breathed on them and said to them, 'Receive the Holy Spirit'" (20:21–22).

One gift of mutual abiding is a sharing in Jesus' joy, "so that my joy may be in you, and that your joy may be complete" (15:11). We participate in that joy in several ways, "It is the result of experiencing God's love that is in Jesus, of being loyal to Jesus' words (*hrēmata*), and of reflecting the glory of God to the world."[22] There is also an eschatological dimension since joy is an experience of eternal life now (16:22).

An incident from the life of Catherine of Siena illustrates the dynamic of mutual abiding and bearing fruit. Catherine spent several years in a solitary room within her family home. Here she experienced deep, mutual abiding with Christ. After her Espousals, i.e., a mystical exchange of hearts with Christ, she longed to spend the rest of her life being wrapped in God.

21. Kanagaraj, *'Mysticism' in the Gospel of John*, 269.
22. Ibid., 270.

However, she learned through prayer that Christ had other plans for her. Her biographer, Raymond of Capua, writes,

> our Lord began, little by little, to lead on Catherine to mingle with other people, but unobtrusively and with disciplined restraint. At the same time he did not deprive her of his own divine companionship; but rather . . . he favoured her with it in an even more abundant measure than before.[23]

During prayer, Catherine heard Christ speak to her, "Leave me now. It is dinner-time and your family are sitting down to dinner; go and join them; and afterwards you can come back to me."[24] However, Catherine wept when she heard these words and she lamented,

> Sweetest Lord, why are you driving me away from you? . . . But spare me the bitter punishment of being even for a moment separated in any way from you. What does mealtime mean to me? I have food to eat of which they to whom you are sending me know nothing. . . . None knows better than yourself how I have turned my back on human companionship in order to find you, my God and my Lord. And, unworthy as I am, by your mercy I have found you, and by your graciousness I have made you my possession.[25]

Nonetheless, in her weeping, Catherine heard,

> Dearest daughter, let it be so for this occasion, for so it is right for you to fulfil *all* justice; for my grace in you must now begin to bear fruit not only in your-

23. Raymond of Capua *The Life of Catherine of Siena* part 2, chap. 1, sec. 120.

24. Ibid.

25. Ibid.

self but in other souls as well. I have no intention
whatever of parting you from myself, but rather of
making sure to bind you to me all the closer, by the
bond of your love for your neighbour. Remember
that I have laid down two commandments of love:
love of me and love of your neighbour. 'On these
two commandments,' as I myself bore witness, 'de-
pend the Law and the Prophets.' It is the justice of
these two commandments that I want you now to
fulfil. On two feet you must walk my way; on two
wings you must fly to heaven.[26]

Catherine left her seclusion and spent many years attending to the poor and victims of the Black Plague as well as
serving as a mediator for the warring Italian city states and re-
storing the papacy by bringing back the pope from Avignon.

Appropriation

This chapter has two related challenges for us as the beloved
in God's household. It focuses on the heart of Christian living
by describing how disciples are related to Jesus and the Father
in three dynamic relationships. It also develops how these mutual relationships of knowing, loving, and abiding affect our
lives in God's household with others who are God's beloved.
See chart 3.2 above, **The Life of God's Beloved**, to review the
model of mutual relationships.

Look back now on the *Reflection Questions* and your responses. Then review *Critical Inquiry of Christian Tradition*.
What new connections do you see? Write them down.

Next, review your *Appropriation* from chapter 2. How
did you visualize the mutual relationships of the Father and

26. Ibid., sec. 121.

Jesus by an abstract or concrete sketch with some colored markers or a collage? Can you now add details to visualize how disciples are related to Jesus and the Father? To one another in the household of God? Is a new graphic called for?

Share your connections about the chapter and the drawing with one other person or in a small group. What do the connections and drawings say about your life? Do others have similar experiences? How do newspapers and magazines confirm or contradict your shared experiences?

Another way to *appropriate* what you are learning is to do it contextually. To what situation can you bring your learning? Recall a recent conversation within your family, in the neighborhood or at work. Reflect on the possibilities relating your learning to the next time you are in conversation.

You may enjoy movement, singing, playing a musical instrument, writing lyrics or poetry. How could your learning be expressed?

Try some way of *appropriation* before going to the next chapter.

---4---

The Activities of God's Beloved

Hearing and Keeping Jesus' Words
for Oneself and God's Household

Noise accompanies us day and night. No matter where we are and what we are doing, our ears function as antennae for our minds and hearts. They are filters for what accompanies us on our daily journey. How do we differentiate the sounds? What takes precedence? Children's cries, beeps on computers, brakes screeching in traffic, protest rallies, cheering crowds? Music, wind, rain, thunder, ocean waves? How do we distinguish the authoritative sounds of words? Advertisements, conversations, song lyrics, sermons, political speeches, voice mail? Often we feel an urgency to respond immediately. Occasionally, there is time and space for reflection.

Words can startle, challenge, and bless us. Each day we can choose to become perceptive hearers of Jesus' voice. It is a spiritual discipline to know what to listen to, what to retain in our minds, hearts, and imagination. What words will accompany us on our journey as God's beloved? What words can be treasured in God's household? This chapter addresses how Jesus' words direct us and others for daily living in God's household.

Reflection Questions: First Naiveté

1. Describe a recent experience of hearing another person and letting the communication dwell in your mind and heart.

2. During one day, there are multiple experiences of hearing and listening. How do you know which words to keep and which to discard?

3. What was your discernment process in 1 and 2?

4. How does God speak to you? List five ways. Notice how many ways include words.

Critical Inquiry of Christian Tradition

Hearing and Keeping Jesus' Words for Oneself and God's Household

Hearing (*akouō*) and keeping (*tēreō*) Jesus' words is an activity in tandem with believing in him, as well as knowing, loving, and abiding in him. In Jesus' day, words were very important. How individuals listened gave them the opportunity to respond (challenge-riposte) and address the situation of honor or shame for their household. Since there were neither an instantaneous playback of the words nor secretaries, how people heard was very important. The active gossip network also needed interpretation. Persons often evaluated words or speeches according to the authority of the person who was speaking.

How did individuals respond to words? One way was to use the opportunity to maintain or restore the household honor. There was also the possibility of dismissing the words since they were not important to the well being of the household. A third way was to internalize the message as instruction and blessing for daily life. Believers in Jesus took his message seriously,* and it became part of their distinctive way of responding to him and others. Conversely, the foil characters dismissed his message since Jesus had no real authority. This group was more interested in his origins and how to discredit him, since they did not know where he received his training as a rabbi. They were also suspicious of his observance of the Sabbath, his companions, the persons whom he met and with whom he conversed. Jesus observed Jewish tradition, but he also was convinced that some cultural and religious boundaries needed reform.

Hearing and Keeping Jesus' Word/s in the Book of Signs

After Jesus heals the paralytic on the Sabbath (5:1–9), he speaks to the Judeans (*hoi Ioudaioi*) in a monologue (vv. 19–47). This is the first time that "hearing" and "believing" are closely related, "Anyone who hears my words and believes him who sent me has eternal life" (v. 24). An anonymous crowd also hears differently. Some hear Jesus with understanding because of their belief, while others are restricted to a physical hearing of Jesus' word because of their implied lack of faith (7:40–42). Hearing Jesus' words clearly divides them (7:43).

In chapter 8, Jesus and the Judeans are engaged in a vigorous, challenge-riposte dialogue. While some believe in him (vv. 31–33), others do not. Jesus states his own identity with God that enables him to hear the Father's words, whereas "you do not hear them (because) you are not from God" (v. 47). Kinship with Jesus (and the Father) is not possible for those who do not believe in him. Thomas Aquinas offers additional reasons for not hearing Jesus' words when he cites Gregory. There are persons who cannot physically hear the words. Others who hear cannot embrace them in their hearts. Still others receive the words, and when troubles and pleasures allure them, they cannot keep the words.[1] We may be hearing the parable of the sower and the seed in these reasons (Matt 13:1–23 par.).

In contrast, Catherine of Siena was nourished by the Word throughout her entire life. In one of her numerous letters, she challenges her sons:

> Let your mind's eye be opened to see, and unplug
> your ears and listen to the teaching he gives you
> . . . . To this wonderful school, then, my sons! For
> this energy and love will lead you on and will be
> your life![2]

At the conclusion of chapter 8, Jesus and the Judeans (*hoi Ioudaioi*) continue their challenge-riposte dialogue. When the Judeans accuse Jesus of having a demon, he defends his speech and the honor of his household, "I do know (*oida*) him (the Father) and I keep (*tērō*) his word" (v. 55).

Remember the parable of the Good Shepherd that we discussed in the previous chapter? There the image of "hear his voice" (10:3–4) suggests more than a physical hearing of the shepherd's voice. The sheep respond by following him

1. Thomas Aquinas *Commentary* 2, §63.
2. Letter T226, quoted in Noffke, *Catherine of Siena,* 45.

alone because they recognize him. In the midrashic expansion of the parable, hearing Jesus' voice is necessary to shape one fold (v. 16). The foil characters cannot belong to the shepherd because they refuse to believe and listen to his voice as disciples (vv. 26–27a). Only the one who believes (being of the truth) can listen to Jesus' voice (18:37).

At the conclusion of the Book of Signs, Jesus is speaking to the Judeans (*hoi Ioudaioi*) about believing in him. He summarizes his mission:

> I do not judge anyone who hears my words, and does not keep them, for I came not to judge the world, but to save the world. The one who rejects me and does not receive my word has a judge; on the last day the word that I have spoken will serve as judge, for I have not spoken on my own, but the Father who sent me has himself given me a commandment about what to say and what to speak. (12:47–49)

Jesus only speaks and acts on what he has learned in being nestled at the Father's heart (1:18).

Hearing and Keeping Jesus' Word/s in the Book of Glory

In the Book of Signs we note how each chapter offers different possibilities for believing in Jesus. Narrative scenes, the *sēmeia*, John the Baptist, Jesus' words and works and the witness of the Father develop and are strengthened by the contrast of the literary-theological presence of the foil characters (chapter 1). Those who believe in Jesus enter into a life with him and the Father of dynamic, mutual knowing, loving, and abiding (chapter 2). This life also develops in the household of believers (chapter 3).

Hearing and keeping Jesus' words becomes a major focus in the Book of Glory that is addressed to the disciples of Jesus. The setting for chapters 13–17 is the Last Supper in the Upper Room. The narrator surprises us with unexpected details about Jesus' meal with the disciples (chapter 13). We listen for directions about preparations of the meal. There are none (cf. Matt 26:17–19; Mark 14:12–16; Luke 22:7–13). We anticipate a description of food and the ritual blessing of bread and wine to which Jesus adds new significance and instruction. They are omitted (cf. Matt 26:26–29; Mark 14:22–25; Luke 22:15–20). We are puzzled because we remember that there were abundant meals including wine (2:1–12), fish, and bread for a multitude with twelve baskets of bread fragments left over (6:1–14), and anointing of Jesus' feet with costly perfume (12:1–8).

What details does the narrator offer us about the Last Supper? Jesus takes the initiative in speaking and acting on behalf of his disciples. He speaks about his imminent betrayal (13:10–11, 18–19, 21, 26–27, 37) that begins his return to the Father (13:1, 3). Jesus freely participates in his betrayal, suffering, and death to continue his love for his own to the end (13:1). The one who betrays him is the one who receives the morsel of friendship from Jesus (13:26). When Judas goes out into the night to betray him (13:30), he rejects the light of the world (8:12).

Peter, another one of the Twelve, will also betray Jesus (18:17, 25–27). In this scene, however, he is unwilling to have Jesus wash his feet. When Peter protests, Jesus challenges him: "Do you not want to participate in my life, Peter?" (13:6–8). He does not understand that the washing is a symbolic, prophetic ritual that foreshadows Jesus' suffering and death. If Peter is to share in Jesus' hour of death and new life, he needs to submit to the washing. With bravado, he offers Jesus his head and hands and feet (13:9).

The foreboding announcements about betrayal as well as the foot washing anticipate Jesus' declaration of his imminent departure from the disciples (13:33). As we know, he offers them *one* challenge: "I give you a new commandment, that you love one another. Just as I have loved you, you also should love one another. By this everyone will know that you are my disciples, if you have love for one another" (13:34–35).

An integral part of the Last Supper is Jesus' legacy for the disciples. Consider John 14–16 as a dynamic feast of instruction, i.e., hearing and keeping Jesus' words. Just as Jesus taught the disciples and crowds after the feeding on the hillside (6:1–51), so now he consoles, challenges, and promises a complex future for believers. The setting is really *outside* of time and space and *inside* the hearts of Jesus and the disciples. Although the dialogues and images of the Book of Signs (1:19—12:50) reappear here, the serene setting is jarred neither by the consistent reference to chronological and spatial time nor by Jesus' declarations of suffering.

Jesus' commitment to multiple relationships is the basic conviction of his instruction. How the relationships are extraordinarily connected offers disciples food for a lifetime. Imagine, with the first disciples, how Jesus' departure and return to the Father affects the present and future of all who believe in him. It is Jesus' relationship to the Father, the only Son, who lives at the Father's heart (1:18), which impels him to leave the disciples (13:1; 16:28). Jesus goes to prepare a "dwelling place" for his own (14:2). The separation, however, is only temporary (14:2).

We listen as Jesus promises his disciples: "I will come again and will take you to myself, so that where I am, there you may be also" (14:3). Jesus' one desire for them and for us is that believers may permanently abide with him by sharing in the intimate life that he enjoys with the Father. The theme of Jesus' departure and return is like a picture frame that surrounds his instruction to the disciples (14:2–3; 16:22). Jesus concludes with an extraordinary promise: "I will see you again, and your hearts will rejoice, and no one will take your joy from you" (16:22).

What legacy does Jesus offer to the disciples? His instruction develops in exchanges with them in a three-part sequence: Jesus' revelation, a disciple's question, and Jesus' clarification. The dialogical pattern that is prominent in the Book of Signs continues here. The disciples' misunderstanding of Jesus' teaching prompts the questions to which Jesus responds. Rich irony marks the exchanges for the attentive reader. The disciples' questions attract our imagination and stimulate our hearts, too.

After Jesus announces his departure and return (13:2–3), he encourages the disciples: "And you know the way to the place where I am going" (14:4). However, Thomas is perplexed. Earlier, when the Jews had been ready to stone Jesus, Thomas had been willing to go with him to Lazarus' house, even if it meant death for him (11:16). Now, Thomas misunderstands Jesus. He asks, "Lord, we do not know where you are going [destination]. How can we know the way [route]?" Jesus responds to both questions. First, he is the *way* because he is the *truth*. Jesus reveals to the disciples all that he has experienced of the Father. He is also the *life* because he offers believers a sharing in the intimate life he experiences as God's Son. Second, Jesus' destination is the Father. Jesus reminds the disciples: "You know him and have seen him" (14:7).

"Well, then, Lord," Philip exclaims, "show us the Father and we will be satisfied" (14:8). Philip's request is the third misunderstanding. He desires a direct vision of the Father. Now, Philip had been a disciple of Jesus from the beginning. He had responded to his call (1:43) and invited Nathanael to seek him (1:45). On the hillside, he had known that six months' wages were not enough to feed the crowd that had gathered (6:6). Later, he accompanied Greeks who wanted to see Jesus (12:21). Is it puzzling to the reader that a disciple who had been with Jesus from the beginning could be so imperceptive? Again, Jesus clarifies by repeating the significance of the disciples' experience: Seeing him *is* seeing the Father (14:9). He urges them: "Believe me that I am in the Father and the Father is in me" (14:11, 20).[3]

In chapter 14, the invitation to love (*agapaō*) Jesus by keeping (*tēreō*) his commands appears four times in its positive and negative forms (vv. 15, 21, 23, 24). The invitation indicates that keeping Jesus' commands is not a theoretical component of being a disciple. It means being willing to love one another as Jesus loves us (13:34–35).

Then, Jesus' teaching on love continues without any questions from the disciples. He introduces the image of the vine and branches (15:1–11). We hear, "I am the true vine" (vv.

---

3. Interpretation of John 13–17 appeared earlier in my "Gifts, Challenges, and Promises," 75–80.

1, 5). The wonderful relationship between Jesus, the Father, and believers consists of vine, vinegrower, and branches (vv. 1–2). Pruning (*airei*) or cleansing (*kathairei*) promotes fruitful branches (vv. 2–3). Here the disciples are assured that they are already cleansed "by the word that I have spoken to you" (v. 3b).

Thomas Aquinas offers us several spiritual meanings for this phrase that contemporary scholars do not consider:

> The word of Christ . . . cleanses us from error by teaching us. For the word of God by its power moves our hearts, weighed down by earthly things, and sets them on fire. When God is invoked in baptism . . . this word of faith is so strong in the Church that it even cleanses infants . . . when it is proclaimed from the faith of those who believe, offer, bless and touch the infants. The word of Christ cleanses by the power of faith.[4]

Abiding in Jesus, in his words, is another example of how the disciple participates in mutual abiding (15:7a). How do Jesus' words abide in the beloved? For Thomas, the abiding is active. It consists of "loving, believing, meditating, and accomplishing them."[5] Disciples not only internalize Jesus' words but also they accomplish them, "bear much fruit" (v. 8b). By abiding in Jesus' love, the disciples keep his commands (vv. 9b–10a). Again, hearing and keeping Jesus' words by abiding is not for oneself but for others via personal witness.

Another powerful image in chapter 15 is the analogy of friendship (vv. 12–17): "No one has greater love than this, to lay down one's life for one's friends" (v. 13). Jesus' decision

---

4. St. Thomas Aquinas *Commentary* 2, §1987.
5. Ibid., §1995.

to freely lay down his life in love, for friendship, is the ultimate model for the disciples' mutual loving (15:12–14). Jesus
has made known to them as friends everything that he has
heard from the Father (15:15). Friends resemble one another
in their thinking, speaking, and acting. Jesus, as beloved Son
and teacher, exhorts the disciples to be children of the Father
and servants who are willing to follow their teacher's example
(13:14–16; 15:20).

What will motivate the disciples to live in mutual love
and be servants of all? Will they be able to withstand the
hatred and persecution of nonbelievers? How will they remember Jesus' instruction about persecution from synagogue
members (16:1–3)? Jesus' departure will benefit them. He will
send the Advocate, the Spirit of truth, who will guide them
(16:5–7, 13).

It is the "little while" of Jesus' presence and absence that
stirs up questions among the disciples. Now, they do not question him directly. However, Jesus knows that they are anxious
in pondering the "little while." He asks them (16:16–19) if
they are asking questions! He assures them that their weeping
and mourning and pain will be temporary. Like a woman who
gives birth to a child, their joy will be great when they see
Jesus again (16:20–22).

Finally, Jesus promises to speak plainly, not in parables,
to the disciples about the Father when the hour comes (16:25).
The reference is to the time after Jesus' resurrection when
they will understand his revelation. Immediately, the disciple
chorus responds, "Yes, now you are speaking plainly, not in
any figure of speech" (16:29). Their ironic acclamation, however, will alter in the experience of Jesus' suffering and death

when "you will leave me alone" (16:32). Nevertheless, Jesus' final moment of instruction offers them hope: "In the world you face persecution. But take courage; I have conquered the world" (16:33).

John 17 is Jesus' ultimate legacy, his last will and testimony, to those who have gathered around the table. It goes beyond the farewell speeches of Moses, Joshua, David, and later heroes in Jewish history. The disciples had heard fragments of Jesus' prayer during his public ministry (11:41–42; 12:27–28), and Jesus had instructed them about praying to the Father (14:13–14; 15:7; 16:23–24, 26). Nonetheless, he had never given them the prayer of his heart. Listening to Jesus' prayer happens when we are resting on the breast of Jesus as beloved disciples (13:23). There we hear the beloved Son who reviews his ministry as well as asking for his needs and the disciples' needs. The prayer is a model of requests, thanksgiving, and conviction:

> Father, the hour has come; glorify your Son so that the Son may glorify you. . . . I glorified you on earth by finishing the work that you gave me to do. So now, Father, glorify me in your own presence with the glory that I had in your presence before the world existed. (17:1, 4–5)

Jesus as the Beloved Son recalls the glory he shared with the Father before his sojourn on earth. He knows that he has been faithful to teaching his Father's revelation and continuing his work. As Son, Jesus freely and lovingly embraces his imminent hour, i.e., his suffering, dying, rising, returning to the Father. However, Jesus acknowledges that he can do nothing by himself: "Father, glorify me" (vv. 1, 5).

Next, Jesus remembers how he gave the Father's words to the disciples; and they believed in him. Jesus had protected and guarded the disciples. Now, it is the Father's turn to protect and guard the disciples from the evil one while they are in the world (vv. 11–12, 15). Jesus does not hesitate to intercede for the disciples. He knows his relationship to the Father: "All mine are yours, and yours are mine; and I have been glorified in them" (v. 10). Jesus' confidence is rooted in the intimate mutual life that he shares with the Father and desires for the disciples, "so that they may be one as we are one" (v. 11).

Jesus does not ask the Father anything for the disciples that he has not experienced. When he prays, "Sanctify them in truth; your word is truth" (v. 17), he is aware of its personal cost. Jesus will lay down his life "so that they also may be sanctified in truth" (v. 19). Again, as the Father sent Jesus into the world (1:10–12), so he sends the disciples into the world (17:18). The prayer anticipates Jesus' commissioning of the disciples and gifting them with his spirit on Easter evening (20:21–22).

Finally, Jesus prays for those who will believe in him through the disciples' word and witness (17:20), "that they may all be one. As you, Father, are in me and I am in you, may they also be in us . . . I in them and you in me, that they may become completely one . . . may [they] be with me where I am" (vv. 21a, 23a, 24a). Jesus' petition is not only for unity among believers but also with him and the Father. Hearing and keeping Jesus' words is an ongoing task that is also a catalyst for others. It is the witness of disciples in word and deed that invites others to believe.

Appropriation: Second Naiveté

This chapter takes seriously how we as disciples hear, i.e., listen to words around us. It challenges us as readers to develop personal strategies from both parts of the Gospel to enable us to treasure Jesus' words in order to bear witness to them with our lives. In looking at the Book of Glory, especially, we hear challenges of how to be faithful as beloved of God when Jesus' presence is promised through the Advocate, the Spirit. A description of the Holy Spirit is not developed in the preceding chapters except to hint of her presence on Easter evening. We will consider the Holy Spirit in the next chapter.

Look back now on the *Reflection Questions: First Naiveté* and your responses. Then review *Interpretation of the Stories: Critical Inquiry of Christian Tradition*. What new connections do you see? Write them down.

Next, review your *Appropriation* from chapter 3. How did you visualize the connections of mutual relationships of the Father and Jesus with the disciples? The disciples with one another? Did you engage in contextual connections? Tell stories?

In light of this review, what would be a creative way of sharing what you learned in this chapter? Can you connect with the previous chapters? Does it need to be considered by itself? Try to share your discoveries and insights with at least one other person or a small group.

Again, do some contextual work by listening to others' experiences. Be aware of any connections locally in your neighborhood, church, and market place.

Try some way of *appropriation* before going to the next chapter.

The Activities of God's Beloved

*Seeking and Finding Jesus for
Oneself and God's Household*

Seeking and finding are two essential activities that embrace our physical, emotional, and spiritual lives. Sometimes we are aware of looking for a regime that will give us strength and range of motion for our bodies. At other times we are seeking a lost item or a distant friend. We also occasionally find that what we were searching for was there all the time if we would slow down and make spiritual connections in the midst of our fast-paced and multi-tasking lives.

This chapter is similar to the previous one in that it calls attention to be mindful of particular attitudes that accompany our spiritual lives. Seeking and finding Jesus gives breadth and depth to our daily lives of becoming God's beloved in the company of friends. Several stories, as well as Jesus' teaching, invite us to seek and find Jesus for our well being. The chapter also explores how seeking and finding Jesus through the gift of the Spirit and participation in the sacraments of Baptism and Eucharist are integral to living in God's household.

Reflection Questions: First Naiveté

1. Describe a recent experience of seeking or searching for something or someone that was essential to your life.

2. Focus on how you conducted the searching. Did you ask others for assistance? How long did you search? Was the finding worthwhile? Was the searching/discovering an experience that occurs frequently in your life? Occasionally? Only once? Why?

3. What was your discernment process in 1 and 2?

4. How do you seek God on a daily basis? Occasionally? Frequently? Describe the seeking in a drawing, symbol, or descriptive paragraph.

5. How do you find God on a daily basis? Occasionally? Frequently? Describe the seeking in a drawing, symbol or a descriptive paragraph.

6. Reflect on the importance of seeking/finding God in your life. Was there a particular time in your life when the activity was intense? A peaceful experience? Again, describe the experience that was significant in your life with a drawing, symbol, or descriptive paragraph.

Critical Inquiry of Christian Tradition
Seeking and Finding Jesus for Oneself and God's Household

Jesus, the disciples, and the foil characters are actively involved in seeking (*zēteō*) and finding (*heuriskō*) one another.

We remember stories from our earlier study. The first words of Jesus in the Gospel are a question addressed to two disciples of the Baptist about what they are seeking (1:38). Later, Jesus also questions the Judeans (*hoi Ioudaioi*) about their seeking (7:19). They respond to him (7:20) and address one another with questions about seeking (7:25). In the Passion Narrative, Jesus asks Judas, soldiers and police about whom they are seeking (18:4, 7; cf. v. 8). Finally, as an inclusion with chapter 1, Jesus addresses a question to Mary Magdalene about her seeking (20:15).

Jesus' awareness that others are seeking him is indicated by his statements to the foil characters and the disciples: "You will seek me" (7:34, 36; 13:33). In the Gospel the authorities' seeking of Jesus is frequently recorded (e.g., 5:18; 7:1, 30; 8:36, 40; 10:39; 11:8), whereas the crowd's seeking (6:24, 26) and Pilate's seeking (19:12) occur fewer times.

Other statements also indicate that Jesus finds the man born blind after a deliberate seeking (9:35). The disciples and Pilate find Jesus in the sense of a relational possibility that is based on observation and/or reflection (1:41b, 45b; 18:38; 19:4, 6). The crowd and foil characters are also actively involved in finding Jesus for different reasons (6:25; 7:34, 35, 36).

Objectives for Seeking and Finding Jesus

While disciples and foil characters seek and find Jesus, what distinguishes them are their objectives and motivations. The Jews are the subjects of most seeking and finding constructions. The common people are designated as the "crowd" (*ochlos*) that is a neutral term in the Gospel. Their objective in seeking Jesus is mentioned in only one narrative. His multiplication of bread draws them to him (6:24, 26). Understanding only the physical significance of the sign (*sēmeion* [6:14]), the crowd seeks bread from him again. Insight for the spiritual significance of the sign, which Jesus explains later (6:35–50), is lacking. Finding Jesus (6:25) specifies only the location of his physical presence.

The religious authorities, however, identified thirty-eight times as "the Jews" are a hostile group who seek Jesus in order to kill him (e.g., 5:18; 7:1, 25). Pilate, another authority figure, represents a different type of response. His seeking to know about Jesus leads to a desire to free him (19:12) because an examination motivated Pilate to declare Jesus' innocence (18:39; 19:4, 6).

In contrast to the characters described above, the disciples seek Jesus with other objectives. See chart 5.1 on the following page, **Living as God's Beloved: Seeking and Finding Jesus** (Individual and Communal Paradigms). In the narrative about the call to become disciples (1:35–51), two disciples of the Baptist are drawn to his witness to follow after Jesus (vv. 35–37). Jesus takes the initiative in their first encounter by asking them about their seeking. They, in turn, ask where he lives and he invites them to find out (v. 38). The verb "live" (*menō*) (vv. 38–39) connotes the double sense of lodgings and the abiding that is characteristic of Jesus' relationship to the Father and the disciples. The experience of dwelling with Jesus leads to a series of discoveries about his identity, which the disciples proclaim with increasing awareness and insight. Their witness about Jesus is a series of christological titles, "Messiah" (v. 41), "the one about whom Moses wrote in the Law and the Prophets" (v. 45), "the Son of God and King of Israel" (v. 49).

CHART 5.1
Living as God's Beloved:
Seeking and Finding Jesus

Individual and Communal Paradigms	Sacramental Paradigms: Baptism	Sacramental Paradigms: Eucharist
A witness testifies about Jesus to an individual whose experience of Jesus leads the individual to witness to another. • John invites Andrew and "other" disciple • Andrew invites his brother, Simon • Philip invites Nathanael • Woman of Samaria to townspeople *Jesus calls an individual to follow him.* • Philip *Jesus and an individual dialogue* • Nathanael • Nicodemus • Woman of Samaria *Witnesses to one another* • Townspeople of Sychar • Risen Jesus and community of believers (and to Nicodemus)	**John 3:1–21** **Being born from above/born again of water and the Spirit** (vv. 3–8) gives **eternal life** to everyone who **believes** (vv. 14–15). The **individual** lives by **acting in the light** with deeds clearly rooted in God (v. 21). **John 4:1–42** *A spring of water gushing up to eternal life* (v. 14) **John 13:4–11** Jesus poured water into a basin, washed his disciples' feet and wiped them with a towel (v. 5). Peter protests. Jesus responds with a negative challenge: Unless I wash you, you have no share with me (vv. 6–8). If I washed your feet, you ought to wash each other's feet (v. 14).	**John 6:1–14** **A crowd coming** to him (v. 5). **Jesus took loaves, gave thanks, distributed loaves and fish** as much as they wanted (v. 11). **When they were filled,** he told his disciples: **Gather up the fragments** left over, so that nothing may be lost (v. 12). Unlike the Synoptic Gospels (Matthew, Mark, and Luke), the Fourth Gospel does not describe an institution account at the Last Supper. Rather, in John 13:1—17:26, the narrator describes the foot-washing event, Jesus' dialogues with the disciples, his monologues, and his prayer to the Father. There are indications, however, in another context (John 6:51–58).

Note: This visual chart offers readers an understanding of the ongoing seeking and finding of Jesus through one another and the sacraments of Baptism and Eucharist.

Their confession draws others to Jesus who encounters the individuals personally (vv. 40–42, 43–50).

The disciples' understanding of Jesus' identity, however, is transcended by his self-proclamation as "Son of Man," the one in whom the Father's glory is revealed (v. 51). The paradigm of discipleship at the beginning of the Gospel functions as a symbol to unfold the possibilities of being disciples, which are revealed throughout the Gospel.

Please refer to chart 5.2 on the following page, **Post-Resurrection Scenes in John** 20. The risen Jesus' encounter with Mary Magdalene is the epitome of the seeking/finding activity of the disciples. Although all four Gospels mention Mary Magdalene in scenes before and after Jesus' resurrection, only the Fourth Gospel highlights her as the one woman at the tomb. The Synoptic Gospels have post-resurrection scenes that are similar in setting and instructions to John 20:1–18. However, the distinctiveness of the Johannine tradition is evident from the inclusion of one female (Mary Magdalene) and one male character (Jesus) who speak with different emphases (cf. Matt 28:1–8; Mark 16:1–8; Luke 24:1–10).

Let us draw near to the garden where Jesus was buried. Notice that in 20:1–18 there are two distinctive scenes that are dependent upon each other (vv. 1–10, 11–18). In the first scene, Mary Magdalene who had stood near the cross of Jesus (19:25), comes to the tomb and sees that the stone was rolled back (v. 1). Immediately, she runs to Simon Peter and the Beloved Disciple and reports her loss, "They have taken the Lord out of the tomb, and we do not know (*ouk oidamen*) where they have laid him" (v. 2). It is not clear if she expects them to assist her in the search to find Jesus' body.

Mary Magdalene disappears, and we can focus our attention on Simon Peter and the Beloved Disciple who are

CHART 5.2
Post-Resurrection Scenes in John 20.

John 20:1–2 (A)	Setting	John 20:11–18 (A')
"Early, first day of week," "dark," outside tomb of Jesus		Outside the tomb
"Mary Magdalene" (v. 1)	Characters	"Mary Magdalene," "angels," "a gardener"
What will she do? The stone was removed.	Conflict	Who are the angels? Can they respond to Mary's weeping? (vv. 12–13). Who is the gardener? Can that character provide assistance? (vv. 14–15)
Mary Magdalene runs to Simon Peter and the other disciple, the one whom Jesus loved and announces: They have taken away the Lord out of the tomb, and we do not know where they have laid him (v. 2).	Denouement	Mary sees angels sitting where the body of Jesus had been (v. 12; cf. 20:6–8).
		They ask, "Woman, why are you weeping?"
		She responds, "They have taken away my Lord, and I do not know where they have laid him" (v. 13; cf. v. 2).
[John 20:3–10 (B)]		"Mary" sees the "gardener" (v. 14).
Setting. Inside the tomb		He asks: "Woman, why are you weeping? Whom are you seeking?"
Characters. "Peter and the other disciple"		She responds, "Sir, if you have carried him away, tell me where you have laid him, and I will take him away" (v. 15).
Conflict. Who is the other disciple, the one whom Jesus loved? Why did that disciple let Peter enter the tomb first? (vv. 4–6a). What did Peter see? (vv. 6b–7). What did the other disciple see? (v. 8). What did they understand about Jesus? (v. 9).		Jesus says, **Mary.**
		She said, "Rabbouni" (v. 16).
		Calling one another is a mutual knowing and recognition of relationship.
Denouement. The identity of the other disciple, the one whom Jesus loved and that one's relationship to Peter are not explicit. Peter sees Jesus' burial wrappings in different places. The other disciple saw and believed. Cf. narrator's comment (v. 10).		"Jesus" commissions "Mary" to proclaim the good news to my brothers and sisters, "I am ascending to my Father and your Father, to my God and your God" (v. 17).
		Fictive kinship transforms natural kinship.
		"Mary" announces to the "disciples, **I have seen the Lord**" (v. 18).

Note: The chart follows the narrative design of other charts. An addition is the ABA' pattern that draws attention to the similarity of AA' and their relationship to B. The literary structure is identified as a chiasm.

principal characters in the scene. Both run toward the tomb, but the Beloved Disciple arrives first and peers into the tomb. However, he waits to enter until after Simon Peter arrives and enters. There they find the linen cloths and the head napkin that are lying in separate places (vv. 3–7). While neither disciple speaks, the Beloved Disciple "saw and believed" (v. 8). The narrator comments, "for as yet they did not understand the scripture, that he must rise from the dead" (v 9). When the disciples return home, there are no characters in the garden area (v. 10).

The second scene confirms Mary Magdalene's earlier discovery (vv. 11–18). Does it present anything new for us? It depends on how we understand what the Beloved Disciple "saw and believed" (v. 8) as well as the narrator's comment (v. 9). The Beloved Disciple is an intuitive, close friend of Jesus. Remember how he rested on Jesus' bosom at the Last Supper? He dared to ask about the identity of the betrayer (13:23–25). At the foot of the cross, Jesus gave him and his mother new, mutual relationships (19:26–27). Here, however, if the Beloved Disciple grasped the mystery of Jesus' resurrection, would the disciples return to their homes? The accounts in the Synoptic Gospels do not suggest indifference to Jesus' resurrection. Rather, the disciples leave the tomb and go out to witness to others (Matt 28:8; Luke 24:10). The Beloved Disciple's "seeing and believing" is not a confessional genre. It is limited to noticing the empty tomb and the burial clothes in different places. In addition, when we look for the characterization of call and response, we find that it is missing. Simon Peter denied Jesus' call and did not respond to him after he denied him three times in the courtyard (18:15–17,

25–27). Although the Beloved Disciple had stood faithfully at the cross (19:25–27), he had not heard the voice of the risen Jesus. There can be no response without a prior call.

When Mary Magdalene re-enters the scene, the plot resumes. While she is weeping, she stands outside the tomb and then peers inside it (v. 11). Two angels are seated where the body of Jesus was. We are surprised, too, since the disciple found only burial wrappings in the same place. By describing the precise position of the angels, the narrator emphasizes why Mary is searching. When the angels ask her why she is weeping, she repeats the same statement that she gave to the disciples (vv. 12–13).

Turning around, she sees Jesus but does not recognize him. Jesus echoes the angels' question and adds, "Woman, why are you weeping? Whom are you seeking (*zēteis*)?" Assuming that he is the gardener, Mary Magdalene speaks about her search again: "Sir, if you have carried him away, tell me where you have laid him, and I will take him away" (vv. 14–15).

Mary Magdalene engages in three conversations while she is trying to find Jesus' body. Her weeping and the loss of Jesus' body are consistent elements in her announcements to the disciples, angels, and Jesus (vv. 13–15). Since she misunderstands his identity, Jesus takes the initiative to end her search. He calls her by name, "Mary," and she recognizes him as her teacher, "Rabbouni" (v. 16; cf. 10:4). In knowing both Jesus' absence (vv. 2, 13, 15) and his presence, Mary clings to him (v. 17). If the scene concluded here, there would be a clear pattern of call and response. The scene would mirror two other encounters where Jesus addresses the same question to two followers of the Baptizer and the crowd in the garden:

"What [or Whom] are you looking for?" (1:38; 18:4). One group responded by following Jesus while the other group seized him for crucifixion.

Although there is a denouement of mutual recognition between Jesus and the woman, what follows surpasses any expectations of Mary Magdalene and us when reader. Jesus commands her, "Do not hold on to me, because I have not yet ascended to the Father. But go to my brothers (and sisters) and say to them, 'I am ascending to my Father and your Father, to my God and your God'" (v. 17).

By connecting his resurrection to the ascension, Jesus indicates that his relationship to Mary Magdalene (and all believers) will be different. His return to the Father, to be where he dwells, is another moment of the hour in which he is glorified. The theological, rather than the chronological and spatial intention, of v. 17 also indicates a new relationship that the disciples will enjoy with the risen Jesus and the Father. Jesus' hour of glorification enables the disciples to be children of the Father, and brothers and sisters of Jesus.

The familial language of "children," "brothers," and "sisters" does not designate persons who are under parental care as dependents. Rather, the terms identify adult believers who belong to the household of God. Jesus, the Beloved Son, is the archetype of what it means to be a son or daughter of God and in relationship with others. Jesus enjoys dynamic living with the Father that is characterized as mutual knowing, loving, and abiding. Being a disciple of Jesus invites persons to that dynamic living.

When we analyze the final verses of this scene (vv. 17–18), we notice a parallel to the witness of the resurrection in the Synoptic Gospels (Matt 28:7–8; Luke 24:6–9; cf. Mark 16:8). However, there are two differences in the Johannine account. First, the message of Jesus is about resurrection-ascension and new relationships (v. 17). Second, Mary Magdalene is the sole witness to the apostles, "Mary Magdalene went and announced to the disciples, 'I have seen the Lord'; and she told them that he had said these things to her" (v. 18).

The dynamic of Jesus and Mary Magdalene is a clear illustration of call and response in climatic sequence. First, Jesus addresses her as "woman" (v. 13), a courteous greeting (cf. 2:4; 19:26). Next, he calls her by name, "Mary," that enables her to recognize him personally. Finally, he claims her as his "sister" in the family of God whom he addresses intimately as "Father." The narrator identifies Mary Magdalene as an "apostle" according to Pauline criteria that recognize an experience of the risen Jesus and a commission to preach the good news (1 Cor 15:3–11). As the first witness of the resurrection, Mary Magdalene responds to Jesus' new calling. She fulfills her commission by identifying Jesus for the disciples with new understanding.

Similarly, Mary Magdalene calls Jesus by different names. First, she addresses him as "Sir," a respectful greeting (v. 15). Next, she identifies him as "Rabbouni" (v. 16), a name with which the disciples address Jesus (1:38, 40; 4:31; 9:2; 11:8). Finally, she names him "Lord" (v. 18), similar to Thomas' recognition: "My Lord and my God" (20:28).[1]

There are two additional post-resurrection narratives in chapter 20. The second one occurs the same evening (vv.

---

1. The interpretation of John 20 appeared earlier in my "Resurrection of the Lord," 589–91.

19–23). The setting is stark. Anxious disciples cower behind a locked door. They are bound together by fear of the Jews (v. 19a). Taking the initiative, Jesus appears and offers them his peace and presence (vv. 19b–20a). Recognition of Jesus happens when he shows the disciples his hands and side (v. 20a). Fears fade into the shadows of the waning day as they rejoice in his return (v. 20b). He assures them that they are not orphans (cf. 16:22) and offers them not only an unimaginable gift but also a responsibility.

Like the previous scene, Jesus commissions them, "*as* the Father has sent me, *so* I send you" (v. 21). In this verse we hear the pattern of Jesus' knowing, loving, and abiding with the disciples. The source and intensity for the relationships is his mutual relationship with the Father (10:15; 15:9; 17:21a).

Jesus' mission of proclaiming God's truth becomes their mission. They are charged to continue Jesus' revelation of the Father. They are challenged to live out their decision to believe in Jesus by loving one another as Jesus and the Father love both one another and the disciples (15:9, 12b).

How will they accomplish this witness and task? Jesus breathes upon them and says, "Receive the Holy Spirit. If you forgive the sins of any, they are forgiven them; if you retain the sins of any, they are retained" (20:22–23). Jesus' hour has now been definitively completed. He has returned to renew his relationship to the disciples by meaning of commission, the insufflation of his Spirit, and directives to be reconcilers. There is no indication of the disciples' immediate response to Jesus' appearance (v. 20).

In the third scene (20:26–29), eight days later, when Thomas sees Jesus' wounds, he changes from a skeptic to a believer. After seeing and touching him, Thomas believes in him and witnesses to him, "My Lord and my God" (vv. 27–28). His witness (and the other disciples) is a consistent challenge to believers (vv. 30–31).[2]

Motivations for Seeking and Finding Jesus

The crowds, Pilate, the authorities, as well as the disciples seek/find Jesus according to their basic decision to believe in him. The crowd that seeks Jesus in 6:22–24 does not understand his signs (*sēmeia*) in v. 25. In their dialogue with Jesus (vv. 26–34) they do not understand his instruction about the heavenly bread because they do not believe in him. Rather, they challenge him to prove his authority by always giving them bread (v. 34). The crowd only wants his generosity as a bread provider. Pilate, too, has an opportunity to hear the truth (18:37), to become a believer. Although he desires Jesus' release, he capitulates to the Jews (19:16). In contrast, the authorities seek to destroy Jesus because they believe neither in his claims to work on the Sabbath nor his relationship to the Father (10:33; see 5:18; 7:21–24, 28–30).

However, the disciples' believing in Jesus is the basic motivation for seeking him. We remember that two disciples of the Baptist begin to believe in Jesus because of his witness (1:35–37). Immediately, they encounter Jesus who inquires about their seeking and invites them to share his dwelling (1:38–39). Consequently, their belief in him becomes the basis for witness to others who also become disciples (1:40–50).

2. The interpretation of John 20:19–29 appeared earlier in my "Son of Man," 73.

The ongoing task of seeking/finding Jesus is also supported by experiencing the mutual relationships of knowing, loving, and abiding in him. While dwelling with Jesus is emphasized as the object of the disciples' searching, knowing, and loving him are components of seeking his identity, especially in relationship to the Father.

The foil characters, however, never experience Jesus at this level because they do not believe in him. They have no desire to share his life or his dwelling. In the literal sense, their seeking/finding of Jesus reaches a climax in the garden where he takes the initiative and asks them about their seeking (18:4, 7). "Jesus the Nazarene" is their repeated reply (vv. 5, 7). Jesus responds to their question with "I am he" (egō eimi) (vv. 5–6, 8). Now, the words can be interpreted literally. Nonetheless, readers know that the name is used theologically throughout the Gospel (e.g., 4:26; 9:9; 10:11; 11:25). Although they physically apprehend Jesus, they do not find him at a deeper level. Their lack of faith in him means they do not seek/find him as the source of life; rather, they seek to destroy him and the life-giving power that he offers to those who believe in him.

At this point, readers may wish to review from chapter 1, the mysterious figure of Wisdom whom the Johannine community drew upon to create the hymn to the Word (1:1–18). Wisdom is also the inspiration for the seeking/finding paradigm of this chapter. Raymond F. Collins identifies discipleship as "the search for incarnate Divine Wisdom."[3] In the Hebrew Bible and the Septuagint, there are three dynamic characteristics of Wisdom. First, Wisdom invites an individ-

3. Collins, "The Search for Jesus," 37.

ual to seek her (Prov 8:1–4). Second, mutual relationships develop in that Wisdom and the individual seek and find one another (Wis 1:1–2, 6:13; Prov 1:20, 3:13, 8:17). Third, Wisdom gives her blessings: knowledge (Proverbs), presence of God (Job); meaning and continuity of life (Ecclesiastes, Sirach).[4]

The Spirit in the Fourth Gospel

The gift of the Spirit on Easter evening is the culmination of her descriptions and promises in the Gospel. Initially, John the Baptist witnesses to his disciples about Jesus. He is the one upon whom "the Spirit (*to pneuma*) descends and remains (*emeinen*)" (1:32). Readers recognize baptismal references in Jesus' dialogue with Nicodemus. He testifies, "No one can enter the kingdom of God without being born of water (*hudatos*) and the Spirit (*pneumatos*)" (3:6; cf. v. 8). At the conclusion of Jesus' speech, we hear, "He whom God has sent speaks the words of God, for he gives the Spirit (*to pneuma*) without measure" (3:34).

Next, we hear in Jesus' conversation with the woman of Samaria about authentic worshipers of "the Father in spirit and truth (*ēn pneumati kai alētheia*), for the Father seeks such as these to worship him. God is Spirit (*pneuma*), and those who worship him must worship in spirit and truth (*ēn pneumati kai alētheia*)" (4:23b–24).

Finally, in the midst of the Feast of Tabernacles, Jesus cries out,

> Let anyone who is thirsty come to me, and let the
> one who believes in me drink. As the scripture has

4. Pazdan, *Discipleship*, 297–304.

> said, "Out of the believer's heart shall flow rivers
> of living water (*hudatos zēntos*)." Now he said this
> about the Spirit, which believers in him were to
> receive; for as yet there was no Spirit, because Jesus
> was not yet glorified. (7:37–39)

Here we see not only the connection between water and the
Spirit but also how believers will receive the Spirit after Jesus'
hour of glorification.

The role of the Spirit becomes clearer in the Book of
Glory. Here we remember (chapter 4) the setting of Jesus' last
instruction to the disciples (chapters 14–16). Jesus promises
them "another Advocate (*paraklēton*) to be with you forever"
(14:16). The very next verse offers strength and consolation to
the disciples and to us:

> This is the Spirit of truth (*to pneuma tēs alētheias*)
> whom the world cannot receive because it neither
> sees him nor knows him. You know him, because
> he abides (*menei*) with you, and he will be in you.
> (14:17)

A few verses later the narrator connects "Advocate" with
"Holy Spirit" and offers the functional role of the Spirit in
the lives of believers: "But the Advocate (*paraklētos*), the Holy
Spirit (*to pneuma to hagion*), whom the Father will send in
my name, will teach you everything, and remind you of all
that I have said to you" (14:26). The Spirit teaches and recalls
for us everything that Jesus heard nestled at the heart of the
Father. The verb "remind" (*hupomnēsei*) does not function
as a static, automatic communication; rather the Spirit is a
dynamic presence whom believers can call upon to remember
what Jesus heard and taught.

A similar function of the Spirit occurs in 15:26, "When the Advocate (*paraklētos*) comes, whom I will send to you from the Father, the Spirit of truth (*to pneuma tes alētheias*) who comes from the Father, he will testify (*marturēsei*) on my behalf." We remember studying the witnesses to Jesus: John the Baptist, Jesus' words and works, the Father and the Scriptures (chapter 1). In 15:26 the Spirit enables the witnesses to speak to believers by reminding them of the Gospel.

In chapter 16, there are two additional references to the Holy Spirit. In 16:7b–8, we hear, "I tell you the truth: it is to your advantage that I go away, for if I do not go away, the Advocate (*paraklētos*) will not come to you; but if I go, I will send him to you." The last reference about the Spirit is related to the earlier ones. In 16:13, we read,

> When the Spirit of truth (*to pneuma tēs alētheias*) comes, he[5] will guide you into all the truth (*en tēi alētheiai pasēi*); for he* will not speak on his own*, but will speak whatever he* hears, and will declare to you the things that are to come. He* will glorify me, because he* will take what is mine and declare it to you.

This theology of the Holy Spirit is unique among the Gospels and the Letters of Paul. It is based upon the mutual, dynamic life of Jesus and the Father. The activity of the Spirit is integrally connected to how Jesus and the Father continue to be related to one another and the disciples after Jesus' resurrection. The Spirit's roles, i.e., abiding, teaching, and recalling

5. While the NRSV translates the pronoun *ekeinos* as "he," the Greek can easily be rendered "that one." Since to personalize the Holy Spirit as "he" is not beneficial theology, I have marked with an asterisk all the places in these verses where the pronoun can be translated "that one."

what Jesus has taught, express how believers will experience Jesus and the Father. The extraordinary promises of Jesus at the Last Supper are fulfilled in the lives of believers after his hour of glory. Disciples can experience "a full understanding of the mutual presence of Jesus and the Father in one another, a full understanding of the mutual presence of Jesus and the disciples in one another, and the assurance of 'living' as Jesus himself 'lives.'"[6]

Baptism in the Fourth Gospel

While seeking and finding Jesus are personal and communal experiences, so is baptismal initiation. References to "water" and "light" are major theological symbols in the Gospel. See chart 5.1 above, **Living as God's Beloved: Seeking and Finding Jesus** (Sacramental Paradigms: Baptism). In addition to the conversation between Jesus and Nicodemus about the necessity of being baptized to enter the reign of God (3:5), there is the responsibility of those who believe in Jesus, "But those who do what is true come to the light, so that it may be clearly seen that their deeds have been done in God" (3:21). In addition, Jesus proclaims his self-identity as the light of the world (8:12). The story of the man born blind (chapter 9) employs light and the ritual of washing in the pool of Siloam (v. 7).

Another pericope whose symbol of water functions on multiple levels is Jesus' conversation with the woman of Samaria (chapter 4). Jesus' promise of "living water" (*hudōr zōn*) in verse 10, as well as his teaching in 7:38, is ordinarily interpreted as baptism or the Holy Spirit. We know from our

---

6. Segovia, *The Farewell of the Word*, 108.

study that the multivalent character of Johannine language precludes one meaning.

While the narrator identifies "living water" as the Holy Spirit, there is an additional comment, "as yet there was no Spirit, because Jesus was not yet glorified" (7:39). The statement connects baptism/Holy Spirit to Jesus' hour. Later, we see that Jesus is washing the disciples' feet (13:4–11). He says to Peter, "Unless I wash you, you will have no share (*meros*) with me" (13:8). Baptism flows from Jesus' freely chosen death. Unless we are willing to be initiated into the suffering and death of Jesus, we do not share in his resurrection-life. Jesus' example of service is also a model for our way of living in the household of God.

Interpreters often identity the blood and water flowing from Jesus' side (19:34) as the birth of the church, i.e., the household of God. The symbol refers to Jesus' death as well as the sacraments of initiation, Baptism, and Eucharist. Catherine of Siena comments,

> Bleeding from every member, he has made himself cask and wine and cellarer for us. Thus we see that his humanity is the cask that encased the divine nature. The cellarer—the fire and the hands that are the Holy Spirit—tapped that cask on the wood of the most holy cross. . . . we should take the wine of his indescribably thirty desire for our salvation, and give it back to him in the person of our neighbor.[7]

Thomas Aquinas identifies the blood and water as a prefigured event, "for just as from the side of Christ, sleeping on the cross, there flowed blood and water, which makes the

---

7. Letter T136/G36/D737, in Noffke, ed., *The Letters of Catherine of Siena*, 1:142–43.

church holy, so from the side of the sleeping Adam there was formed the woman, who prefigured the Church."[8]

Eucharist in the Fourth Gospel

As we remember, the Synoptic Gospels offer a common narrative of the Last Supper that highlights the ritual blessing of bread and wine to which Jesus adds new significance (chapter 4). In the Fourth Gospel, however, after Jesus gets up from the table (13:4) to wash his disciples' feet, he gives instruction, and prays to the Father. Some interpreters suggest that the Last Supper narrative is so well known to the Johannine community that there is no need to mention it again. Others indicate that the symbols of meals, bread, wine, and vine identify the Eucharist[9] just as our discussion of Baptism includes water and light. Another group states that the Gospel was even anti-sacramental since there are no "overt references" to the sacraments.[10] Our study, however, indicates that the Gospel is profoundly symbolic and uses ordinary things (e.g., water, light, bread) for our senses, minds, and hearts to appropriate on many levels.

Concern about adequate food and drink begins early in the Gospel. Recall the wedding feast at Cana (2:1–11). Compare the request of the woman of Samaria, "Sir, give me this water, so that I may never be thirsty or have to keep coming here to draw water" (4:15), with the disciples who had gone into town for food (4:8). When they returned, they were worried about Jesus eating (4:31–38).

8. Thomas Aquinas *Commentary* 2, §2458.

9. Brown, *Introduction*, 230.

10. Ibid., 231.

Later, Jesus feeds the crowd on the hillside (Matt 14:13–21; Mark 6:32–44; Luke 9:10–17; John 6:1–15). The activity is often compared to the Last Supper and the Eucharist in the life of the Church. Please refer to chart 5.1 above, **Living as God's Beloved: Seeking and Finding Jesus** (Sacramental Paradigms: Eucharist). When we investigate the Johannine account of the feeding, however, we find three differences. First, the setting is "the Passover, the festival of the Judeans, was near" (6:4). For several decades scholars have reconstructed the season and ritual of Passover during Jesus' lifetime to identify it with accounts of his Last Supper with the disciples. A survey of the Gospels indicates that while references to Passover are limited to Jesus' last meal with his disciples in the Synoptic Gospels, many Passover references are connected with Jesus' activities in the Fourth Gospel.

In the Book of Signs, Jesus goes up to Jerusalem to cleanse the temple (2:14–22) when the Passover is near (2:13), and remains there during the festival (2:23–25). Again, the Passover is near (6:4) when Jesus feeds the multitude on the hillside (6:5–15). After he raises Lazarus from the dead, crowds go up to Jerusalem to purify themselves for Passover (11:55), while six days before the feast Jesus goes to the home of Lazarus in Bethany (12:1–8). In the Book of Glory, Jesus' meal with his disciples occurs before the festival of Passover (13:1–11). John 13–17 may be Jesus' commentary on the Passover meal[11] while John 18:28—19:44 narrates preparations for the feast.

Second, Jesus takes the initiative for the feeding as well as taking the loaves, giving thanks, distributing them (and the fish) for abundant eating (6:4–11). The crowd recognizes Jesus

11. Laufer, "The Farewell Discourse," 147.

as a prophet (Deut 18:19) because they see his sign (*sēmeion*) and want him for their king (6:14–15).

Third, the narrative is followed by the Bread of Life discourse wherein Jesus instructs the crowd about the significance of the feeding (6:35–58). The dialogical structure of the discourse material begins when the people question Jesus about his new location (v. 25). Jesus' response evaluates their insufficient understanding, "Very truly I tell you, you are looking for me, not because you saw signs, but because you ate your fill of the loaves" (v. 26). He challenges them to work for "food" that will never perish, which the Son of man will provide (v. 27).

The narrative moves rapidly from being fed on the hillside (v. 11) and seeking the bread giver (v. 26) to asking about how to do God's work (v. 28). Jesus assures them that doing God's work is to believe in the one whom God has sent (v. 29). In seeking assurance, they ask him what sign he will offer them to authenticate himself as someone grater than Moses who pleaded with God for bread in the desert. The narrator implies that the crowd does not remember the feeding (vv. 30–31). Jesus states that it was not Moses but his Father who gives the true bread for the life of the world (vv. 32–34).

In v. 35 we hear the climactic statement of revelation that the remaining verses clarify and extend. Jesus identifies himself as the bread of life that satisfies all hunger and thirst for the one who believes in him (v. 35). Immediately, the people who are certain that he is "Jesus, the son of Joseph" dispute his claim. How can he be the one "come down from heaven?" (v. 44). Verses 35–50 are often identified with Jesus' teaching that sustains believers (v. 42) through the Holy Spirit who recalls to them everything that Jesus made known to them (14:26). In these verses the roles of the Father, e.g., giving persons to Jesus (6:37a) and willing all persons to come to him, are integral to Jesus' revelation (v. 39; cf. v. 65).

Verses 51–58 are often identified with a Johannine understanding of the Eucharist. The crowd challenges Jesus, "How can this man give us his flesh to eat?" (v. 52). Jesus' riposte consists of four solemn declarations, "Unless you eat the flesh (*tēn sarka*) of the Son of Man and drink his blood (*to haima*), you have no life in you" (v. 53). Then he restates this truth, "Those who eat my flesh and drink my blood have eternal life, and I will raise them up on the last day" (v. 54). A third time he teaches the profound reality of the feeding, "For my flesh is true food (*sarx mou alēthēs estin pōsis*) and my blood is true drink (*to haima mou alēthēs estin posis*)" (v. 55). Finally, Jesus declares, "Those who eat my flesh and drink my blood abide in me (*en emoi menei*), and I in them. Just as the living Father sent me, and I live because of the Father, so whoever eats me will live because of me" (vv. 56–57).

Thomas Aquinas linked the celebration of the Eucharist to the crucified and risen Jesus. This connection sustained and challenged Thomas. He understood that the Eucharist enables believers to become the Body of Christ. Here are a few verses of his "Sequence for the Feast of Corpus Christi":

> Sing, my tongue, the Saviour's glory,
> Of his flesh the mystery sing:
> Of the blood all price exceeding
> Shed by our immortal King,
> Destined for the world's redemption
> From a noble womb to spring.

What He did at supper seated,
Christ ordained to be repeated,
In his memory divine;
Wherefore we, with adoration,
Thus the Host of our salvation
Consecrate from bread and wine.
They, too, who of Him partake,
Sever not, nor rend nor break,
But entire their Lord receive.
Whether one or thousands eat,
All receive the self-same meat,
Nor the less for others leave.
Here, beneath these signs are hidden
Priceless things, to sense forbidden;
Signs, not things are all we see—
Flesh from Bread, and Blood from wine,
Yet is Christ in either sign,
All entire confess'd to be.

Oh blessed banquet,
Wherein Christ is received.
His Passion is again with
Us, the soul o'erflows
With grace: a pledge
Of future glory is given to us[12]

In addition, in the Office of Readings for the Feast, we find a section from one of his homilies:

O banquet most precious! . . . Can anything be more excellent than this repast, in which not the flesh of goats and heifers, as of old, but Christ the true God is given us for nourishment? What more wondrous than this Holy Sacrament! In it bread and wine are changed substantially, and under the appearance of

12. Chegwidden, "Corpus Christi and St. Thomas."

a little bread and wine is had Christ Jesus, God and perfect man. In this sacrament sins are purged away, virtues are increased, the soul is saturated with an abundance of spiritual gifts. No other sacrament is so beneficial. Since it was instituted unto the salvation of all, it is offered by the Church for the living and the dead, that all may share in its treasures.[13]

Later, Catherine of Siena recognizes Jesus' presence in word and food when she prays to the Trinity,

You, Eternal Trinity, are table and food and waiter for us. You, eternal Father, are the table that offers us as food, the Lamb, your only-begotten Son. He is the most exquisite of foods for us, both in his teaching, which nourishes us in your will, and in the sacrament that we receive in holy communion, which feeds and strengthens us while we are pilgrim travelers in this life. And the Holy Spirit is indeed a waiter for us, for he serves us this teaching by enlightening our mind's eye with it and inspiring us to follow it.[14]

Appropriation: Second Naiveté

In this chapter we explore a major theme of the Gospel. Seeking and finding Jesus for oneself and in the company of friends is part of our daily journey. Sometimes our objectives and motivations can be observed in the believing characters of the Gospel. Other times, they are aligned with the foil characters. The presence of the Holy Spirit, participation in Baptist and Eucharist as well as attentiveness to Jesus' teaching equip us for all that we need as the beloved of God.

13. Ibid.
14. Catherine of Siena *Prayers* 102–3.

Look back now on the *Reflection Questions: First Naiveté* and your responses. Then review *Interpretation of the Stories: Critical Inquiry of Christian Tradition*. What new connections do you see? Where does your heart draw you? To the characters? The descriptions of the Holy Spirit, Baptism, Eucharist? Write them down.

Next, review your *Appropriation* from chapter 4. How can you visualize the activities of God's beloved: hearing and keeping Jesus' Words for oneself and in God's household? How does your imagination include seeking and finding Jesus? Draw, sketch, or cut out pictures from newspapers and magazines to represent the connections.

What would be a creative way of sharing what you learned in this chapter? Can you connect with the previous chapters? Does it need to be considered by itself? Try to share your discoveries and insights with at least one other person or a small group.

Again, do some contextual work by listening to others' experiences. Be aware of any connections locally in your neighborhood, church, and market place.

Finally, what medium can you use to indicate the *appropriation* of the book?

Conclusion

This book considers how our basic identity as God's beloved is described in the Fourth Gospel. We trace its characteristics, beginning with the call to be disciples and to believe in Jesus. Then, we ponder the dynamic life of Jesus and the Father that is expressed in mutual knowing, loving, and abiding. As disciples, we are initiated into that life and appropriate it in God's household by attending to the model of Jesus and the Father. As disciples we also hear and keep Jesus' words and seek and find him in daily life.

A contemporary Australian scholar, Dorothy Lee, writes convincingly of the power of the Gospel for contemporary spirituality. She declares,

> What the Fourth Gospel challenges is the center of the self located solely in either self-preoccupation or relationship with others. The Johannine Gospel sees the source of true identity—in a theological rather than psychological sense—as friendship with God: an interior meeting of heart to heart that becomes an abiding-place, a strong and stable locus for self-knowledge and self-giving love within the context of the community of faith.[1]

1. Lee, *Flesh and Glory*, 195.

Jesus is the beloved who offers us all that we need to become the beloved of God, too. Our study includes characters who believe in Jesus, as well as the foil characters that choose not to believe in him. As we study and live out this Gospel, we find ourselves as mirrors of different characters. Some appeal to us; others we disregard. Much depends on the seasons of our hearts and our spiritual journey.

Are there other models that represent being God's beloved? The mysterious character of the disciple whom Jesus loved is another possibility. While scholars in the early and contemporary Christian tradition do not agree on the historical identity of this disciple, we can benefit from a symbolic tracing of the character in the Gospel. As we know from earlier study, the identification, "the disciple whom Jesus loved," appears primarily in the Book of Glory (13:23; 19:26; 20:2; and 21:7, 20, 24). Nonetheless, a few years before his death, Raymond E. Brown questioned whether "another disciple" who followed Jesus with Andrew might be the beloved disciple (1:35–42).[2] I consider the identification of the character as the same one to locate the disciple in both parts of the Gospel. In addition, "another disciple" (*ho allos mathētēs*) is often coupled with "the disciple whom Jesus loved" in the Book of Glory (cf. 18:15, 16; 20:2, 3, 8; 21:2, 7).

When we identify "another disciple" with the Beloved Disciple in the Book of Signs, we are confident that the disciple witnessed everything that Jesus said and did. In particular, we recognize Jesus' challenge to the Judeans (*hoi Ioudaioi*), "If God were your Father, you would love (*ēgapate*) me, for I came from God and now I am here" (8:42), as well as know-

2. Brown, *Introduction*, 338.

ing Jesus' love for Martha, Mary, and Lazarus (11:3, 5, 11, 36). We remember that it was Jesus' raising Lazarus from the dead that was the catalyst for the authorities to plot his death (11:53).

The Book of Glory identifies the Beloved Disciple as the one who has the place of honor at Jesus' breast during the Last Supper and asks about the betrayer (13:25). As a special friend of Jesus, we can imagine the significance of Jesus' teaching on the vine and branches (15:1–11). In *The Dialogue*, which is a conversation between God and Catherine of Siena, we hear,

> You should be like them [my servants], joined and engrafted to this vine. Then you will produce much fruit, because you will share the vital sap of the vine. And being in the Word, my Son, you will be in me, for I am one with him and he with me. If you are in him you will follow his teaching, and if you follow his teaching you will share in the very being of this Word—that is, you will share in the eternal Godhead made one with humanity, whence you will draw that divine love which inebriates the soul. All this I mean when I say that you will share in the very substance of the vine.[3]

God and Catherine also listen to one another about Jesus' command of mutual loving and bearing fruit (15:12–17). She records,

> The same is true of many of my gifts and graces, virtue and other spiritual gifts, and those things necessary for the body and human life. I have distributed them all in such a way that no one has all of them. Thus have I given you reason—necessity, in fact—to practice mutual charity. For I could well have sup-

3. Catherine of Siena *The Dialogue* no. 23, 61.

> plied each of you with all your needs, both spiritual
> and material. But I wanted to make you dependent
> on one another so that each of you would be my
> minister, dispensing the graces and gifts you have
> received from me. So whether you will it or not,
> you cannot escape the exercise of charity! Yet, unless
> you do it for love of me, it is worth nothing to you
> in the realm of grace.
>
> So you see, I have made you my ministers,
> setting you in different positions and in different
> ranks to exercise the virtue of charity. . . . All I want
> is love. In loving me you will realize love for your
> neighbors, and if you love your neighbors you have
> kept the law. If you are bound by this love you will
> do everything you can to be of service wherever you
> are.[4]

We see how these powerful challenges in *The Dialogue* as well as our earlier study of mutual knowing, loving, and abiding coalesce at the foot of the cross. Here, a few persons are gathered around Jesus, namely, "his mother, and his mother's sister, Mary the wife of Clopas, and Mary Magdalene . . . (and) the disciple whom he loved" (19:25–26a). While the soldiers cast lots for Jesus' garments (v. 24), Jesus gazes at his mother and the Beloved Disciple and creates new, mutual relationships, "Woman, here is your son . . . Here is your mother. And from that hour the disciple took her into his own home" (v. 26b).

Unlike the disciple, Jesus' mother appears only at the wedding feast in Cana (2:1–11) where Jesus tells her, "My hour has not yet come" (2:4b). Here she participates in Jesus' hour of suffering and death along with the disciple whose wit-

4. Ibid., no. 7, 38.

ness we can believe. They represent future believers who are given "power to become children of God, who were born, not of blood or of the will of the flesh or of the will of a human person, but of God" (1:12b–13). They are the nucleus of a fictive family, i.e., persons who choose freely to believe in Jesus and form community with one another.

We noticed in the preceding chapter the significance of a soldier piercing Jesus' side after his death. Blood and water came out (19:35). The symbols of Baptism, Eucharist, and the Holy Spirit indicate how the community is sustained in living as the family of Jesus. Catherine of Siena links the vine and branches to the blood of the cross:

> the blood—the life—of Christ and the life of the redeemed have become inextricably one in the mystery of the cross. It is the parable of the vine and the branches . . . of the double engrafting of the Word into humanity and onto the cross, of the vessel of the human heart holding the blood of Christ.[5]

Mary Magdalene is another character whom a few scholars identity with the Beloved Disciple.[6] We noticed in the previous chapter how her development as a character compared to Peter and the Beloved Disciple. Mary Magdalene is entrusted with the proclamation of the resurrection. In particular, the Risen Jesus directs her "to go to my brothers and sisters and say to them, I am ascending to my Father and your Father, to my God and your God" (20:17b). This scene is the culmina-

5. Letter T209/G2 in Noffke, ed. and trans., *The Letters of Catherine of Siena*, 2:299, n. 8.

6. E.g., Pazdan, "Resurrection of the Lord," 588–91; and Schneiders, "Because of the Woman's Testimony," 233–54.

tion of the new family who live as beloved in the household of God.

The Gospel of John is mysterious, challenging, and transforming. It is a solitary, literary witness to becoming God's beloved in the company of friends. Prayer, study, discussion, and living the Gospel extend authority and power far beyond the limitations of the text or a community of believers. We are the witnesses for whom Jesus prays. We are the ones through whom others will come to believe (17:20). We can trust our experience of the mystical union of Jesus and the Father with us, "that they may all be one. As you, Father, are in me and I am in you, may they also be in us . . . I in them and you in me, that they may become completely one . . . may [they] be with me where I am" (vv. 21a, 23a, 24a).

Truly, Catherine of Siena is our model for living as God's beloved in the company of friends:

> Catherine's challenge to us . . . to find nourishment in the Word of the Scriptures as contemplatively as she did. . . . But it is above all to nourish ourselves, as she put it, 'at the table of the cross,' becoming one with the Word, the crucified and risen Jesus, so that our blood like his, will be the seed of the life of God for the world. Then God's truth will be realized in us. Then we will be truly Church.[7]

---

7. Noffke, *Catherine of Siena*, 152–53.

Bibliography

Barrosse, Thomas. "The Relationship of Love to Faith in St. John." *Theological Studies* 18 (1957) 538–59.

Bauer, Walter, W. F. Arndt, F. W. Gingrich, and Frederick W. Danker. *A Greek-English Lexicon of the New Testament and Other Early Christian Literature.* 3d ed. Chicago: University of Chicago Press, 2001.

Béchard, editor and translator. *The Scripture Documents: An Anthology of Official Catholic Teachings.* Collegeville, MN: Liturgical, 2001.

Bieringer, Reimund, et al., editors. *Anti-Judaism and the Fourth Gospel: Papers of the Leuven Colloquium 2000.* Jewish and Christian Heritage Series 1. Louisville: Westminster John Knox, 2001.

Brown, Raymond E. *The Gospel of John.* 2 vols. Anchor Bible 29, 29A. Garden City, NY: Doubleday, 1966–1970.

———. *An Introduction to the Gospel of John.* Edited by Francis J. Moloney. Anchor Bible Reference Library. New York: Doubleday, 2003.

Catherine of Siena. *The Dialogue.* Translated by Suzanne Noffke. Classics of Western Spirituality. New York: Paulist, 1980.

———. *The Letters of Catherine of Siena.* 2 vols. Translated and edited by Suzanne Noffke. Medieval and Renaissance Texts & Studies. Tempe, AZ: Arizona Center for Medieval and Renaissance Studies, 2000–2001.

———. *The Prayers of Catherine of Siena.* Edited by Suzanne Noffke. New York: Paulist, 1993.

Chegwidden, James. "Corpus Christi and St. Thomas." Centre for Thomistic Studies, accessed at http://www.cts.org.au/.

Collins, Raymond F. "The Search for Jesus: Reflections on the Fourth Gospel." *Laval théologique et philosophique* 34 (1978) 27–48.

Dumm, Demetrius R. *A Mystical Portrait of Jesus: New Perspectives on John's Gospel.* Collegeville, MN: Liturgical, 2001.

Howard-Brook, Wes. *Becoming Children of God: John's Gospel and Radical Discipleship.* Bible and Liberation Series. Maryknoll, NY: Orbis, 1994. Reprinted, Eugene, OR: Wipf & Stock, 2003.

Kanagaraj, Jey J. *'Mysticism' in the Gospel of John: An Inquiry into Its Background.* Journal for the Study of the New Testament Supplement Series 158. Sheffield: Sheffield Academic, 1998.

Laufer, Catherine. "The Farewell Discourse in John's Gospel as a Commentary on the Seder Service." *Colloquium* 27.2 (1995) 147–60.

Lazure, Noël. *Les Valeurs morales de la théologique johannique.* Études bibliques. Paris: Gabalda, 1965.

Lee, Dorothy. *Flesh and Glory: Symbolism, Gender and Theology in the Gospel of John.* New York: Crossroad, 2002.

Malina, Bruce J., and Richard L. Rohrbaugh. *Social-Science Commentary on the Gospel of John.* Minneapolis: Fortress, 1998.

McPolin, James. "Johannine Mysticism." *The Way* 18 (1978) 25–35.

Moloney, Francis J. *The Gospel of John.* Sacra Pagina 4. Collegeville, MN: Glazier, 1998.

Noffke, Suzanne. *Catherine of Siena: Vision through a Distant Eye.* Collegeville, MN: Liturgical, 1996.

Nouwen, Henri J. M. *Life of the Beloved: Spiritual Living in a Secular World.* New York: Crossroad, 1996.

Pagels, Elaine. *The Johannine Gospel in Gnostic Exegesis: Heracleon's Commentary on John.* Nashville: Abingdon, 1973.

Pazdan, Mary Margaret, OP. *Becoming God's Beloved in the Company of Friends: A Spirituality of John's Gospel.* Canfield, OH: Alba House Communications, 2003. CDs and Audio Tapes.

———. *Discipleship as the Appropriation of Eschatological Salvation in the Fourth Gospel.* Ann Arbor: University Microfilms International, 1982.

———. "Fifth Sunday in Lent, Year A. Gospel Lesson: John 11:1–45." In *The Lectionary Commentary: Theological Exegesis for Sunday's Texts.* The Third Readings: The Gospels, edited by Roger Van Harn, vol. 3. Grand Rapids: Eerdmans, 2001.

———. "Gifts, Challenges, and Promises in John 13–17." *The Bible Today* 38.2 (2002) 74–80.

————. "Resurrection of the Lord, Years A, B, C. Gospel Lesson: John 20:1–18." In *The Lectionary Commentary: Theological Exegesis for Sunday's Texts*, edited by Roger Van Harn, vol. 3. Grand Rapids: Eerdmans, 2001.

————. *The Son of Man: A Metaphor for Jesus in the Fourth Gospel*. Collegeville: Glazier, 1991.

————. "Thomas Aquinas and Contemporary Biblical Interpreters: 'I Call You Friends' (John 15:15)." *New Blackfriars* 86 (2005) 465–77.

Pontifical Biblical Commission. "The Interpretation of the Bible in the Church." *Origins* 23:29 (January 6, 1994) 497–524.

Raymond of Capua. *The Life of Catherine of Siena*. Translated by Conleth Kearns. Wilmington, DE: Glazier, 1980.

Ringe, Sharon H. *Wisdom's Friends: Community and Christology in the Fourth Gospel*. Louisville: Westminster John Knox, 1999.

Schnackenburg, Rudolf. *The Gospel of John*. 3 vols. Translated by Cecily Hastings et al. New York: Crossroad, 1968–82.

Schneiders, Sandra M. "Because of the Woman's Testimony." In *Written That You May Believe: Encountering Jesus in the Fourth Gospel*. Rev. ed. New York: Crossroad, 2003.

Segovia, Fernando F. *The Farewell of the Word: The Johannine Call to Abide*. Minneapolis: Fortress, 1991.

Thomas, Aquinas, St. *Catena Aurea*. Vol. 4, Part 1: *St. John*. Albany, NY: Preserving Christian Publications, 1995.

————. *Commentary on the Gospel of St. John*. 2 vols. Translated by James A. Weisheipl and Fabian R. Larcher. Aquinas Scripture Series 4. Albany, NY: Magi, 1980.